OPIE DOESN'T
LIVE HERE
ANYMORE

WALT MUELLER

OPIE DOESN'T
LIVE HERE
ANYMORE

WHERE FAITH, FAMILY,
AND CULTURE COLLIDE

Standard
PUBLISHING

www.standardpub.com

Published by Standard Publishing, Cincinnati, Ohio
www.standardpub.com

Printed in the United States of America

Project editor: Robert Irvin
Cover design: Studio Gearbox
Interior design: Edward Willis Group, Inc.

All Scripture quotations, unless otherwise indicated, are taken from the HOLY BIBLE, NEW INTERNATIONAL VERSION®. NIV®. Copyright © 1973, 1978, 1984 by International Bible Society. Used by permission of Zondervan. All rights reserved.

Scripture quotations marked *The Message* are taken from *The Message* by Eugene H. Peterson. Copyright © 1993, 1994, 1995, 1996, 2000 by NavPress Publishing Group. Used by permission. All rights reserved.

"What's Going On" words and music by Marvin Gaye, Al Cleveland, and Renaldo Benson © 1970, 1971, 1972 (Renewed 1998, 1999, 2000) Jobete Music Co., Inc. All rights controlled and administered by EMI April Music Inc. and EMI Blackwood Music Inc. on behalf of Jobete Music Co., Inc. and Stone Agate Music (a division of Jobete Music Co., Inc.). All rights reserved. International copyright secured. Used by permission.

ISBN 978-0-7847-2113-1

Library of Congress Cataloging-in-Publication Data

Mueller, Walt, 1956
  Opie doesn't live here anymore : where faith, family, and culture collide
Walt Mueller.
     p. cm.
  ISBN 978-0-7847-2113-1 (perfect bound)
  1. Family—Religious aspects—Christianity. 2. Popular culture—
Religious aspects—Christianity. 3. Parent and teenager—Religious aspects—
Christianity. I. Title.

BT707.7.M85 2007
261.0973—dc22

                                                          2007001765

13 12 11 10 09 08 07   9 8 7 6 5 4 3 2 1

 # DEDICATION

TO THE GLORY OF GOD, with thanks to him for the wonderful gift of my four children: Caitlin, Josh, Bethany, and Nate. Thanks for loving an imperfect dad, who is still struggling to understand and live out his faith before his family and in his world. I pray that each of you will eagerly embrace the struggle for the rest of your days.

CONTENTS

FOREWORD

ONE OF THE MOST IMPORTANT LESSONS I've learned in youth ministry is that I can't do everything, be everything, and know everything. When it comes to knowing about youth culture, I've learned to trust Walt Mueller to be my guide. Because of Walt and his ministry at the Center for Parent/Youth Understanding, I don't have to try to keep up with everything that's changing daily in youth culture. I've allowed Walt to be my cultural guide, yes, but also my filter and my friend. And he's done it again with *Opie Doesn't Live Here Anymore: Where Faith, Family, and Culture Collide.* In understanding the ever-changing youth culture, Walt has come to my rescue and served me well.

It's crazy, but it wouldn't be surprising if, before the year is out, one of the following cultural forces isn't around anymore: MySpace, MTV, instant messaging, YouTube, Paris Hilton, reality TV, iPods. Cultural issues and products are advancing at a quicker pace than you and I are able to keep up with. And because of this, many youth workers, leaders, and parents are failing to consider how these changes are impacting young lives.

I'm constantly thinking about how caring adults can deal with the realities and challenges of our youth culture while trying to point teenagers to the unchanging love of Jesus. It's not an easy task. Culture is seductive and intriguing and strongly calls on teenagers to follow. What do we do? Well, some avoid the problems and create an isolated bubble of "Christian culture," where we don't talk about or interact with secular issues; we simply label them as "evil." Others give up fighting the monsters of culture and marketing, naively hoping teenagers will navigate their own way without suffering too much harm. Unfortunately, neither approach is helpful in preparing today's teenagers to live by a biblical worldview and to face the challenges of being a follower of Jesus. That's why I'm a fan of Walt's and love his resources. He's not in denial, he's not given up hope, and he's committed to helping people like you and me.

I've known Walt for many years, and I've always appreciated his passion for being a devoted student of culture and deeply committed follower of Jesus. I'm thrilled that you are getting the chance to sit at his feet and glean knowledge from his writings over the past few years. This book, inspired by real events and cultural trends as Walt has watched them unfold in recent years, is a great resource to help you understand how to guide your kids and your students when their faith and culture collide—which is daily. Thanks, Walt, for providing another resource that makes our jobs a little easier!

Doug Fields
Youth pastor, Saddleback Church
President, SimplyYouthMinistry.com

Opie Doesn't Live Here Anymore

 # INTRODUCTION

I GREW UP IN A WORLD that never really existed. I just didn't know it at the time. Sure, there were pains, problems, and difficulties. But loving parents and a happy home in well-manicured suburbia made my childhood and preteen years pretty easy and attractive. When I think back to those days, my memories are all good, and any bad there was has long since been forgotten.

At the time, television's *The Andy Griffith Show*, my favorite childhood program, was not only a black-and-white fantasy land to which I loved to escape, but also somehow the place—known as Mayberry—where I imagined living. Because we shared the same age, freckles, and carefree life, Mayberry's Opie was me. Oh, if only life was so clean, neat, and easy.

Today, I look in the rearview mirror of my life and see that the messy reality of being human has always been there in some way, shape, or form. However, my childhood innocence and simple-minded idealism had combined with the protection of a happy home to eclipse what I now see and understand to have been true not only since the day I was born, but since my earliest ancestors (who, by the way, we all share) decided to do their own thing.

I've come to realize that the innocence of Mayberry is not only long gone—it was never there in the first place.

No matter how much we'd like to think otherwise, Opie doesn't live here anymore. In truth, he was never more than a fictional character who lived on TV.

Since that day in the Garden of Eden, there are three threads that have been woven through every square inch of the fabric of history. I know about them because I've read about how they've touched all of humanity since the day the crafty serpent slithered away from Adam and Eve. And I know about them because they've been pounding away in every square inch and every moment of my own life since the day I was born.

First, everything and everybody is pretty messed up. Sin has affected the very core of our world and our selves. We can see it when we look around at a culture that is changing rapidly—and often not for the good. And, if we're honest with ourselves, we can see it every time we look in the mirror to gaze into the deepest recesses of our own hearts. Something's wrong, and we know it, because we see it around us and within us.

Second, God hasn't thrown up his arms and stepped back, abandoning us to the consequences of our rebellion against him. Instead, he cursed the serpent and, after measuring out the penalties that we had to face as well, threw his arms around us. He's embraced us in his grace, mercy, and love by setting in motion a marvelous unfolding plan to include another chapter in the world's story that follows the ones titled "Creation" and "Fall." The gift of the chapter known as "Redemption" means that the story's ending doesn't have to be empty, hopeless, and sad. Instead, God has undone the mess by reclaiming and rebuilding his kingdom through the God-man, Jesus Christ—the kingdom that will come in all its finality and fullness when he comes again.

And third, you and I aren't here in this time and place by accident. We aren't here just to hang around and wait for our hearts to stop beating or for Jesus to return. We aren't here either to endure in or escape from this world. Instead, God has placed us as his particular people in this particular time and this particular place to live out his will and his way under his reign. As Jesus prayed the night before he died (John 17), that will is that we live out the kingdom in the world while avoiding adopting the ways of the world. As Christ's followers, we're to maintain a redemptive presence in a world that looks nothing like Mayberry . . . and it's a struggle. We're to represent Christ by undoing the mess wherever we can. As the great Dutch statesman and theologian Abraham Kuyper recognized, "There is not a square inch in the whole domain of human existence over which Christ, who is sovereign over all, does not cry 'Mine!'" Our lives should be under Christ's lordship because we have been claimed as his. As a result, our task is to live and proclaim that lordship to every nook and cranny of creation that cries out and groans for redemption (Romans 8:22).

This is a book about the intertwining of these three threads. It is about joyfully embracing the struggle as our faith, our families, our culture, and all of life collide. It's about what it means for God's people and the world to meet.

These pages contain numerous blogs and essays I've written as I've watched these threads intertwine and wrestled with how to integrate Christian faith into all of life. Everything you read has been occasioned by events and circumstances that have caused me to seek to understand what it means for God's kingdom to come—as Jesus taught us to pray—in response to those events and circumstances. And I purposely chose these entries across a number of years to show how, as life and culture changes—rapidly, sometimes frighteningly—my faith has been challenged to grow and adapt along with those changes.

It's my prayer that some of these thoughts bring you great comfort and hope. At other times, I hope to challenge and provoke you (and me) to think more seriously and deliberately about what it means to be a Christian in today's world. If at times you think my critique of the church or how Christians are living might be too harsh, please realize that I include myself as the object of this criticism. I have learned that while God promises me the gift of a peaceful heart, it's equally important to maintain a restless mind. I must look in the mirror to evaluate how well I conform to the image of Christ, not so I can pat myself on the back, but so I am driven to my knees in repentance and humility over my shortcomings.

My life as a husband, father, son, brother, friend, church member, and culture-watcher has been filled with bumps and bruises. Life isn't nearly as simple and clean as I once thought it was. I'm extremely grateful to God for allowing me to experience a life, as John Piper wrote, that has been "a rhythm of need and nourishment" and "a rhythm of danger and deliverance."[1] The thoughts I've recorded in this

Opie Doesn't Live Here Anymore

book flow out of my personal experience of that messy, yet wonderful, reality where our faith, our families, our lives, and our rapidly changing culture collide . . . the place where we both live and belong, making an impact in a way that brings honor and glory to God and God alone.

Walt Mueller
Founder and president
Center for Parent/Youth Understanding (CPYU)
Elizabethtown, Pennsylvania

LOOKING FOR BUS #119— ON YOUTH CULTURE AND MORALS

MY DAD ALWAYS TOLD THE TRUTH.

When I was little, he would impart his frank nuggets of wisdom through a repertoire of often-repeated sayings that imprinted themselves into the stuff I am made of today. If I only had a dollar for each time I heard him say "Privileges come with responsibility," "Money doesn't grow on trees," or my least favorite one, "This is going to hurt me a lot more than it hurts you." Back then, hearing those things was deeply annoying. Still, Dad was telling the truth.

> ## Dad can count his blessings for having parented in an earlier and easier time. I can't.

In recent years Dad has continued to tell the truth. At various times we'll discuss the reality of our changing world, especially the shifting choices, challenges, problems, and expectations facing children and teens. Sometimes when we broach the subject, he looks at me and says, "I'm so glad I'm not raising kids in today's world." This oft-repeated saying of his captures the truth about the differences between the world he raised me in and the world in which I'm raising my kids. It's not easy.

Dad can count his blessings for having parented in an earlier and easier time. I can't. I face that same assignment in a different world. But rather than bemoan my situation, I have to believe that God has blessed me by giving me the opportunity to speak the truth into my kids' lives in today's world.

We can't ignore our present reality. Rather, we must respond. The great theologian John Stott often speaks about the responsibility of the Christian to face reality and to craft a response by engaging in what he calls "double listening." In other words, followers of Christ aren't only to take time to listen to the Word, we're to take equal care in listening to the world. It's only when we have listened hard to our rapidly changing world that we can effectively bring the light of God's Word to bear on these new realities.

As a culture-watcher, this is my calling. Over the years, I've struggled to make sense of the changes taking place. Along the way, I've hoped and prayed that I would be like the "men of Issachar, who understood the times and knew what [people] should do" (1 Chronicles 12:32).

In this section you'll face the sometimes unsettling realities of life for young people growing up in today's world. I trust you'll also hear the unchanging Word that speaks to these realities.

What You See Is What I Am

Youthculture@today, CPYU quarterly newsletter; March 2001

There's a boxful of gorgeous women up in my attic.

I stumbled upon it a few weeks ago while I was up there looking for something else. The box of Barbie dolls, clothes, and accessories brought back memories of the days when my now-teenage girls were young enough to enjoy hours spent quietly playing with dolls.

> Someone once did a little calculating and discovered that if Barbie was a real, live woman, she'd stand at 7' 2" tall and have measurements of 40-22-36.

Like most people, I never thought of Barbie as an educational toy. But while I was reminiscing over the box of Caitlin and Bethany's forgotten plastic friends, I got to thinking about all the controversy poor Barbie has had to endure for supposedly teaching little girls unrealistic lessons about body image and what makes a woman attractive. For more than forty years, Barbie has been held, dressed, undressed, looked at, and played with by three generations of little girls. Barbie's critics tell us that, during that time, millions of girls have unconsciously absorbed appearance standards from Barbie that are even more unrealistic than those nasty arch problems with her feet. (I always felt sorry for her—Barbie was cursed with a foot problem so severe that whenever she kicked off her super-high-heeled shoes, she had to walk around on the balls of her feet.)

Opie Doesn't Live Here Anymore

Someone once did a little calculating and discovered that if Barbie was a real, live woman, she'd stand at 7' 2" tall and have measurements of 40-22-36. Her neck is twice the length of a normal human's neck. Even with some radical foot surgery that might take her height down to 6' 6", she still doesn't come even close to looking like the 5' 4", size 12, 37-29-40, average woman who lives here in North America.

Perhaps there's some legitimacy to the criticism Barbie has received. I've never met a young woman who's felt the pressure to look "average." Our culture is so permeated by an obsession with appearance that we don't even notice how bad and pervasive the problem is.

I remember the first time the issue reared its ugly head for me as a father. I had driven Caitlin to her new school the day before she was to begin kindergarten. It was around 3:30 PM when we arrived there. The older students, who had started school a few days before, were climbing aboard their buses for the afternoon ride home. We got out of the car to head into the school.

> I've never met a young woman who's felt the pressure to look "average." Our culture is so permeated by an obsession with appearance that we don't even notice how bad and pervasive the problem is.

Six-year-old Caitlin's hand was in mine. As she anxiously watched the older students leave, she looked up at me and asked, "Daddy, what if kids make fun of me tomorrow?"

"Make fun of you? For what?" I asked.

Her answer threw me. "For what I'm wearing or for what I look like."

I was dumbfounded. As parents, my wife and I had deliberately worked to downplay this pressure in our home. But somehow, the messages from our appearance-conscious culture had been heard.

Clinical psychologist Mary Pipher, author of the best-selling book *Reviving Ophelia,* has been working for years with girls whose lives are bearing the fruit of this sad pressure. She believes that a "national cult of thinness" has developed in the last two decades. Standards of beauty have not only been defined and communicated by our culture, but they are standards that have become slimmer and slimmer. In 1950, the White Rock mineral water girl weighed 140 pounds and stood 5' 4" tall. Today, she is 5' 10" and weighs 110. Pipher writes:

> Girls compare their own bodies to our cultural ideals and find them wanting. In all the years I've been a therapist, I've yet to meet one girl who likes her body. Girls as skinny as chopsticks complain that their thighs are flabby or their stomachs puff out . . . They have been culturally conditioned to hate their bodies . . . When I speak to classes, I ask any woman in the audience who feels good about her body to come up afterward . . . I have yet to have a woman come up.[1]

But don't think that Barbie's to blame for all this. Our media culture is feeding our kids—both our girls and our boys, young children and older teens—a steady diet of images and body-shape role models through every available outlet. All these messages combine to define a standard of appearance that few will ever reach, but seemingly an entire society is striving to attain.

You may wonder why your children are so consumed with spending time in front of the mirror. The answer is simple. They're trying to measure up to the images

Opie Doesn't Live Here Anymore

they've seen plastered on TV, the printed page, billboards, and many other places. They balance perilously between trying to measure up and the frustrating reality of never measuring up. Five-year-old girls and boys who fret, thinking they're already too fat, may be destined to spend a lifetime of energy and a small fortune pursuing the appearance standards portrayed by pop-culture icons like Britney Spears and Brad Pitt. Once these icons get too old, fat, and wrinkled, someone else will take over as the standard-bearer.

But it's not just our kids. Children and adults alike are living a lifestyle that screams "I am what I look like." A walk through any shopping mall confirms this fact. Have you noticed how many businesses, advertisements, and items of merchandise are sold to improve image and appearance? If we stand back and take a look beneath the surface to see what all this has done to us, it's not a pretty sight.

> We care less about inward character and more about outward appearance as the primary expression of who we are.

First, we care less about inward character and more about outward appearance as the primary expression of who we are. Historian Joan Jacobs Brumberg has traced this change in shifting values through American history. In her book *The Body Project: An Intimate History of American Girls*, she notes how the lives of girls in the nineteenth century were oriented towards "good works." Today, that orientation has shifted to "good looks" as girls have come to view their bodies as the primary expression of their identities. She discovered this shift in the tones of their personal diaries. In her book she includes some telling diary entries. An 1892 entry reads:

> Resolved, not to talk about myself or feelings. To think before speaking. To work seriously. To be self-restrained in conversation and actions. Not to let my thoughts wander. To be dignified. Interest myself more in others.

Contrast that with another girl's 1982 New Year's resolution:

> I will try to make myself better in any way I possibly can with the help of my budget and babysitting money. I will lose weight, get new lenses, already got new haircut, good makeup, new clothes, and accessories. [2]

Second, we despise fatness and idolize thinness. Our boys are expected to have bulked-up, fat-free bodies. Our girls are expected to be skinny and sexy. One girl told our folks here at CPYU that the girls in her high school look up to the women who star in the show *Friends*. "Every woman on that show is unrealistically skinny. But teen girls see those beautiful young women in their late twenties and early thirties and think that that's how sophisticated and alluring women look." She goes on: "More than ever before, I've noticed young males being sucked into obsession with body image." The pressure shapes our self-concepts, desires, and dreams. A seventeen-year-old named Jessica shared her poem, "Catalogues," with Sara Shandler, the author of *Ophelia Speaks: Adolescent Girls Write About Their Search for Self.* Jessica writes:

> *Searching through catalogues*
> *you wish you could order*
> *the bodies not the clothes* [3]

Opie Doesn't Live Here Anymore

Third, because we don't like what we see in the mirror, we're very unhappy. By the time they reach the age of thirteen, 53 percent of American girls say they are unhappy with their bodies. By the time they're seventeen, 78 percent are dissatisfied. Have you noticed how much time kids (both girls and boys!) spend in front of the mirror trying to get things to look just right? Have you noticed how many outfits your son or daughter may try on before settling on one that looks the way they want? And have you noticed how irritable and frustrated they get during the process? Yes, things have changed. Kids a few decades ago did not spend anywhere near the time and energy to get ready before going out the door as kids do today. My mother was constantly stopping me to tell me, "Comb your hair, tuck in your shirt, and pull up your zipper." Today's gnawing body dissatisfaction is well known in the retail business. When she goes into a fitting room to try on jeans, the typical girl will try on fourteen pairs before making a purchase; the guys aren't much different.

> Today's gnawing body dissatisfaction is well known in the retail business. When she goes into a fitting room to try on jeans, the typical girl will try on fourteen pairs before making a purchase.

Fourth, our unhappiness leads some of us to take measures that are drastic, sometimes even deadly. We diet, abuse laxatives, work out excessively, get plastic surgery, and take muscle-building supplements. Some try to cope through eating disorders. Dr. Jean Kilbourne, known for her pioneering work in critiquing advertising images, points out that the obsession starts early. "Some studies have found that from 40 to 80 percent of fourth-grade girls are dieting. Today at least one-third of twelve- to thirteen-year-olds are actively trying to lose weight, by dieting, vomiting, using laxatives, or taking diet pills. One survey found that 63 percent of high-school girls were on diets."[4]

Another study showed that 36 percent of third-grade boys had tried to lose weight. A recent study commissioned by the Girl Scouts of America confirmed that young girls are preoccupied with body image and are trying to do something about it. One fifth-grader quoted in the study says, "I've been counting calories. I'm doing 1,000 to 2,000 calories a day."[5] In 1998, twenty-two thousand American teens had cosmetic surgery—an increase of 95 percent since 1992.

> **Because these disorders often end up as slow suicides, it's not stretching it to say that many young people are dying to be thin.**

Then there is the sad fact of eating disorders—an epidemic closely related to this pressure to be thin and perfect. Today it is estimated that anorexia, the third-most common chronic illness in adolescent girls, occurs in up to 3 percent of all teenagers. Among children, 25 percent of the anorexics are boys. It is estimated that bulimia has personally touched the lives of as many as 10 percent of the young women in America. Because these disorders often end up as slow suicides, it's not stretching it to say that many young people are dying to be thin.

Opie Doesn't Live Here Anymore

And finally, we're learning and living some very sad lessons about a person's value and worth. On the one hand, we make the mistake of failing to see God's image, plan, and purpose in ourselves. On the other hand, we do the same to others. Today's girls feel like they have to look like supermodels to be acceptable to guys. Sadly, our sons grow up with a distorted image of what makes a woman beautiful. The emphasis is not only on outward appearance, but a certain type of outward appearance. In turn, girls view guys by the external standards established in our culture. Nobody measures up, and everyone is disappointed.

A friend recently told me about a Web site she thought I should check out. I was a little concerned about what I was going to find when she gave me the address: www.hotornot.com. What I found was truly unique. Hundreds, perhaps thousands, of people have posted a picture of themselves on the site. Once you look at a picture and rate the subject's appearance on a scale of one to ten, a window pops up telling you the average of all the votes that person has received. It's a sad commentary on what we've become.

Kendall Payne is a young woman who has felt the pressure. A talented singer/songwriter who has come to terms with the battle between inward and outward standards, she's written an incredible song, "Supermodels," that speaks to us all. Among other questions, she asks, *Was it worth the tears you cried to fit the size?* [6]

What we've become is not what we were meant to be. Created with value and worth by a loving God who imparted his own image in each of us, we are people who need to stop idolizing and pursuing the false god of the perfect body. Instead, we must understand that our priority should be the development of inward character. The Scriptures are clear: God is not concerned with outward appearance. Rather, he is concerned with our hearts: "Man looks at the outward appearance, but the Lord looks at the heart" (1 Samuel 16:7). That's the message we should tell the one we see in the mirror—and the message we should pass on to our kids.

Looking for Bus #119

Youthculture@today; March 1998

I speak English and only English. That's why I became increasingly frustrated while standing on a cold, dark, street corner in downtown Prague earlier this year. It was 6:30 AM, I was stumbling under the weight of three bags of luggage, and I had little time to find my way to the airport to catch a plane home. Even *I* was getting sick of hearing myself ask, "Excuse me, do you speak English?" A succession of quick, side-to-side head shakes and confused looks was the only response to my question from a seemingly endless parade of early morning commuters.

All I needed to get started on the long journey home was someone who could understand my question: "Can you tell me where to find bus #119?" After a long period of frustration, a young woman spoke the most beautiful words I had ever heard as a foreign traveler: "Yes, I speak English. You can get on bus #119 down at that corner." Finally, I was on my way home.

While some are consciously aware of it and some are not, those in today's generation of children, teens, and young adults wander through our cultural landscape

Opie Doesn't Live Here Anymore

in search of the Way home. Many of us in the church wonder why their search doesn't lead them enthusiastically into our pews and willingly onto the road to life. Perhaps it's that our unwillingness and lack of enthusiasm—to learn their language and understand their world—is to blame. In other words, it's not a case of this generation consciously turning its back on the church, but the church unconsciously—or maybe even consciously—turning its back on this generation.

Crystal is a twenty-three-year-old university student who cares deeply about the environment. In fact, her environmental science major led her to spend last summer working alongside dozens of like-minded peers as they traveled abroad planting trees. Crystal is also a mature follower of Christ. She cares deeply about the spiritual confusion so pervasive among her peers. She wants to learn their language so she can help them hear the truth. That's why she accepted the challenge of her InterVarsity campus worker and set out on her tree-planting trip to discover as much as she could about her peers and their search for home. While digging holes, she would ask her coworkers, "What do you think about Christ?" Then, she'd just listen.

When Crystal speaks of the educational value of her trip, she isn't necessarily talking about what she learned about the environment. Rather, it's what she learned about, and from, her peers. She told me that she learned three important lessons—ones we must learn also.

First, Crystal found there is no central truth her peers follow. To many of them, everything in life is relative; they have become the first truly postmodern generation. When it comes to religion, they are deeply spiritual. But their searches have led them to create their own personal religions by mixing and choosing a combination of religious elements.

> To many of them, everything in life is relative; they have become the first truly postmodern generation. When it comes to religion, they are deeply spiritual. But their searches have led them to create their own personal religions.

She also learned they are looking for truth everywhere. But when asked about Christianity, they find it repulsive. Why? Because they have rarely, or never, seen real faith in action. What they haven't experienced are relationships with vulnerable people who are truly living God's truth.

Finally, and not surprisingly, Crystal discovered that they want to know about Christ, but don't want anything to do with the church. The issue is not that they have consciously decided never to connect with Christ, but rather that Christ's people have never worked to connect with them. In fact, Crystal's peers see Christians as hypocritical, unreal, and undevoted.

I've had a chance to ponder Crystal's insights for a while now. Her evaluation of her generation is accurate. Unfortunately, her generation's evaluation of the church is too often true as well. This negative opinion of Christ has been shaped not by the God-man himself, but by those called to be his ambassadors in the world.

In his book *Between Two Worlds*, John Stott challenges preachers to become "bridge-builders" by relating the unchanging truths of God's Word to the existential lifestyle of those who long, down deep, to hear Good News. Stott's challenge is relevant to the entire church if we want to effectively communicate to children, teens, and young adults as we enter the new millennium. Stott writes:

> Now a bridge is a means of communication between two places which would otherwise be cut off from one another by a river or a ravine. It makes possible the flow of traffic which without it would be impossible. What, then, does the gorge or chasm represent? And what is the bridge which spans it? The chasm is the deep rift between the biblical world and the modern world. . . . Our task is to enable God's revealed truth to flow out of the Scriptures into the lives of the men and women[7] of today."[8]

Crystal's peers need people of faith who are willing to bridge the chasm. They need to be in relationships with people struggling to relate God's unchanging Word to today's rapidly changing world. They need to be getting directions from people who are unwilling to sacrifice truth to relevance or relevance to truth.

> **Crystal's peers need people of faith who are willing to bridge the chasm.**

Isn't that what Jesus did when he bridged the chasm between Heaven and earth?

I finally caught Bus #119. I made it home because someone took the time to listen to my question, answer my question, and point me in the right direction.

There are a lot of kids wandering aimlessly out there. They're asking questions about how to get home. I doubt they'll find their own way into the church. Will you and

I help them find the Way by taking the body of Christ to them?

Any Kid, Anywhere

Blog; November 15, 2005

Yesterday, a friend called wondering what role, if any, CPYU (the Center for Parent/Youth Understanding) was playing in the unfolding story of the double murder that occurred here in Lancaster County on Sunday morning.

"We're not involved," I replied.

"Well, what do you think of it all?" he asked.

Perhaps the best way for me to sum up my initial thoughts is by simply saying, "Sad, but not surprising." By this time you've no doubt heard about the local eighteen-year-old, David Ludwig, who allegedly shot and killed the parents of his fourteen-year-old girlfriend, Kara Borden. Then Ludwig and Borden took off together, only to be caught yesterday in Indiana.

> The story is loaded with the kind of dramatic twists and turns that make news producers and networks drool. They've been telling the story over and over in typical soap opera fashion.

The story is loaded with the kind of dramatic twists and turns that make news producers and networks drool. They've been telling the story over and over in typical soap opera fashion: a forbidden love affair, a double murder, a kidnapping, insight into their lives through their online blogs, their religious backgrounds, a multistate manhunt,

Opie Doesn't Live Here Anymore

and their history as homeschooled kids. Nonstop network news coverage has featured the "expert" pontificators speculating, as usual, in a manner that tells the story before the story is even known.

To be honest, we've even done a bit of speculating ourselves here at the office. But to pass on our guesses would be a waste of space. Instead, perhaps it's safest to pass on some thoughts that lie beneath my response of "Sad, but not surprising," and how that relates to what we do here every day.

Because the story is local, it's got everybody buzzing. So what's been the buzz in my head? Simply this: It doesn't matter who you and your kids are, where you live, where you work, where you go to church, or where you go to school. You and your kids will be affected by the culture you live in.

Understand that I'm making a general statement that many of you have heard me vocalize for years. My comments aren't specific to this case. I don't know the families, nor do I know enough about their backgrounds to make comments on their tragedy. However, this situation and the specifics as we know them so far have cemented some general thoughts I've had for a long time, thoughts that continue to evolve as I study the Scriptures and observe our Christian subculture.

For years we've been challenging Christian parents to stay in touch with their teenagers and their world. To believe that our faith somehow insulates them from the realities of the world is both pragmatically and theologically wrong. Like it or not, we live in this culture and this culture influences and affects us all. There's no escaping it. There isn't supposed to be. God doesn't want us circling the wagons or living in a bubble in an effort to keep ourselves pure. The God-man, Jesus, prayed the will of the Father the night before his death. That will? That his disciples in all times and in all places would be in the world (living as salt and light) while not of the world (John 17:16-18).

That's not only how we should be living, but how we should be preparing our students to live every day of their lives. Believe it or not, to assume that you've somehow made your kids immune to the influence of culture by shielding them from culture might just produce the exact opposite effect. In other words, by not preparing them to engage the culture with minds and hearts saturated by a biblical worldview, we actually make them more vulnerable to the negative cultural forces they face both now and for the rest of their lives. Both we (parents and youth workers) and our kids need to be wise to the Scriptures and streetwise about our culture. Just as he did with his Son, Jesus, God has made us all particular people who do his particular work in the particular time and place where he's placed us.

> Believe it or not, to assume that you've somehow made your kids immune to the influence of culture by shielding them from culture might just produce the exact opposite effect.

Over the course of the last few months, I've been approached by a growing number of pastors and youth workers who are dealing with a segment of Christian people who resist this approach and even believe it's morally, ethically, and biblically wrong. Sorry, I don't

Opie Doesn't Live Here Anymore

see it. I'm even more sorry for their kids. I love what theologian John Stott says about every Christian's call to become a double-listener: "Christian witnesses stand between the Word and the world, with the consequent obligation to listen to both. We listen to the Word in order to discover ever more of the riches of Christ. And we listen to the world in order to discern which of Christ's riches are needed most and how to present them in their best light."[9]

This is my calling, and the calling of my kids. When it comes to our kids and their culture, what we don't know—or don't want to know, or refuse to know—can hurt them.

SPLITSVILLE

Blog; November 29, 2005

It seems I generated some lively discussion with my November 15 blog, "Any Kid, Anywhere." It's only been a little over two weeks since one of our local kids, eighteen-year-old David Ludwig, became a household name across North America by murdering his fourteen-year-old girlfriend Kara Borden's parents early on a Sunday morning. The story had all the ingredients that make for a great and long-lasting news story in today's world: Older boy loves young girl, both are professing Christian kids, both are homeschooled, both are known by friends as good kids, boy kills girl's parents, and then the two run away together with plans to get married . . .

As I've had the chance to learn more about these kids and their case through ongoing local media reports, some of my initial thoughts and comments about our contemporary youth culture have gelled a bit. Two of these thoughts, in particular, are worth mentioning here.

First, there's the issue of my response when asked, "What do you think of what Ludwig and Borden did?" One blog reader who disagreed with my response of "Sad, but not surprising" was gracious enough to attach a critique that offered the thought that my remark seemed a bit cocky. The reader also stated their own shock and surprise that Ludwig would commit such a crime.

> **One blog reader who disagreed with my response of "Sad, but not surprising" was gracious enough to attach a critique that offered the thought that my remark seemed a bit cocky.**

As stated in my blog earlier this month, any kid, anywhere, anytime is capable of committing such a crime. It doesn't matter how hard we may try to insulate them from the culture and the world, these things (as Jesus said) are rooted deep inside our very beings. For that reason, they are with us all the time—even when we might think that living in a bunker keeps us safe from the world. An understanding of our total depravity and original sin (the latter a doctrine I adhere too) should lead us to be surprised that this type of horror doesn't happen more often.

I thought about this some more when a CNN news crew showed up in our office last week. The young producer and young reporter wanted me to comment for their story, "Who is Kara Borden?" While I refused to offer commentary on specifics related to the case or the two kids—it would only be conjecture on my part—I did

Opie Doesn't Live Here Anymore

offer some general comments about today's youth culture that could shed some light on these tragic events.

Once the cameras were turned off, I continued in a spirited discussion with the reporter and producer regarding the case. There was a question that seemed to haunt them, one I'm sure they had asked many times over the course of the prior week. The reporter looked at me and asked, "How could an eighteen-year-old boy murder two people?!" I wondered out loud why it doesn't happen more. I think I may have scared them a bit when I said, "It's easy for me to understand when I look at the darkness in my own heart." I then attempted to explain the reality of total depravity and the darkness in the human heart. Still, they just couldn't get it.

Their astonishment and disbelief is rooted, I believe, in the fact that, like most in our culture, these two guys, the reporter and producer, had no categories or place in their worldview for original sin or human depravity. To them, human beings are inherently good. If I believed that, then I would have no need for a Savior. I hope and trust that my "Sad, but not surprising" comment isn't rooted in arrogance, but is rooted in my recognition of a humbling reality.

> These two guys, the reporter and producer, had no categories or place in their worldview for original sin or human depravity. To them, human beings are inherently good.

Then there's my second and related thought. It seems that the more we learn about Ludwig and Borden, the more it seems they were simultaneously living at least two separate lives. There was the life each led at home and church. Then there were the other lives they led that have been exposed through their online blogs, Web sites, and Internet conversations. If you've been around me for any amount of time, you've heard me talk at length about the growing phenomenon of "dis-integrated" faith among professing Christian kids. While it's an issue in the entire church, I've focused on kids since I'm so focused on youth culture. It's the problem of professing faith, but not integrating that faith into every area of life. As a result, one can be a "follower" of Christ and still indulge in any number of sinful behaviors. Certainly, that's what happened in this high-profile case.

> **It seems that kids are becoming masters of living a multiplicity of entirely separate lives depending on where they are at the moment. The universe known as the Internet has certainly fostered this reality.**

In a postmodern world, this inconsistency will never be seen as such. But the Ludwig/Borden story reveals another kind of related, yet separate, dis-integration that's growing in today's youth culture. It seems that kids are becoming masters of living a multiplicity of entirely separate lives depending on where they are at the moment. The universe known as the Internet has certainly fostered this reality. And depending on which world you're living in, the people closest to you in that world know virtually nothing about the part of you that lives in the other.

What, then, can you and I take away from all this? First, it's only by the grace of God that we're not sitting in jail cells today. Second, our place is to be in, but not of, the world. We're not only fooling ourselves if we think there's a way to live outside the reality of culture, we're also being disobedient. Third, true faith is integrated into all of life. Fourth, we need to address the growing reality of dis-integration among our kids. And finally, thanks be to God for the gift of his Son.

GOOD-BYE FRANKIE AND ANNETTE

Youthculture@today; March 2004

I was living my mid-1960s childhood when the annual spring break pilgrimage of thousands of college students to Florida's beaches was portrayed on the big screen by teen heartthrobs Frankie Avalon and Annette Funicello. The synopsis of the popular 1965 film *Beach Blanket Bingo* describes how "Bonehead" falls in love with a mermaid, a "not-so-threatening biker terrorizes the beach," and Frankie and Annette surf and sing. Perhaps the most over-the-edge element of the film was Funicello's two-piece bathing suit. I'm sure many members of the older generation of that day were concerned with the film; to them, it must have seemed to provide evidence of a moral slide among the young.

Fast-forward to the spring of 2003. Hundreds of thousands of college students put aside their textbooks and descended en masse on spring break destinations from Florida to Texas to Colorado to Mexico and dozens of other places near and far. But their textbooks weren't all they left at home. In a reflection of how our culture has changed, inhibitions—if there are any—also were left behind as the revelers engaged in a hedonistic free-for-all that made *Beach Blanket Bingo* look like a time capsule of ancient and morally rigid history.

But just like spring break forty years ago, last year's undergraduate fun in the sun had its film version too. But rather than portraying a *Beach Blanket Bingo* fictionalized account of college fun, *The Real Cancun* documents, in reality TV fashion, the adventures of a "wild, hot, and outrageous" group of sixteen students whose attire makes Funicello's four-decade-old two-piece look like a housedress. *The Real Cancun*'s synopsis introduces us to Alan, "a nondrinker and virgin just ripe to be corrupted"; the "lady killer" named Jeremy, who is "always on the prowl"; and the "fun-loving" Roxanne and Nicole—twins with a "knack for stripping." I think back on *Beach Blanket* and can't help but wonder: What were the old people so concerned about?!

> **I think back on *Beach Blanket* and can't help but wonder: What were the old people so concerned about?!**

Perhaps the well-deserved R-rating slapped on *The Real Cancun* best sums up what will be happening over the next few weeks as students descend on spring break destinations near and far. This year's spring break—like the film—will be rated R for "strong sexuality, nudity, language, and partying." With a growing number of college and high school students heading to spring break (and "senior week") destinations, it's imperative we know what's happening when they get there so we can prepare them to make wise decisions, while preventing them from compromising on matters of right and wrong. If our kids and their peers are acting out anything remotely close to *The Real Cancun*, we've got to be concerned. There are

Opie Doesn't Live Here Anymore

several aspects and elements of spring break that warrant our attention and demand a response.

> **Half the men and 40 percent of the women reported drunkenness so extreme that they vomited or passed out at least once during the break.**

First, the underlying philosophy beneath how spring break is both marketed and experienced is basically this: There are no rules. But at this level, spring break is really no different from any other week of the year. Our culture continues to dismiss objective, transcendent standards of right and wrong as hopelessly obsolete. Instead, each and every individual makes a personal decision on what's right or wrong for himself or herself based on how they "feel" at any given moment in time. In addition, there are no inconsistencies or contradictions.

This "do as you please, when you please" ethical system is a surefire recipe for moral anarchy. Many are surprised to learn that even teens and young adults who profess personal faith in Christ don't think twice about doing "whatever I feel like" while on spring break without ever considering that their behavior might be immoral or wrong. When taking part in this weeklong party, it's easy to get caught up in the flow of things and abandon all inhibitions and convictions. That leads to the troubling behaviors that have come to be synonymous with spring break.

Second, there's the drinking. Many spring break tour packages advertise cheap or free alcohol. In a competition for student dollars, one package even includes "50 hours of free drinking!" A recent study done by a major Midwest university found that 75 percent of college men and 44 percent of college women reported being intoxicated on a daily basis during spring break. Half the men and 40 percent of the women reported drunkenness so extreme that they vomited or passed out at least once during the break. A 1998 study from the *Journal of American College Health* found that the average male spring break attendee put away eighteen drinks per day! The average female drank ten. The March 2003 edition of *Teen People* quotes a poll done by a southern university of the 70-plus percent of its students who attended spring break. Of those, 64 percent of the guys and 51 percent of the women got drunk at least once. Twenty percent were either warned or arrested because of alcohol-related behavior. And sadly, drug use is rampant on spring break as well. The drugs of choice tend to be marijuana and club drugs such as Ecstasy.

> **The study done by that southern university found that 42 percent of guys and 22 percent of girls fooled around with someone they met during spring break.**

Third, increased alcohol consumption leads to decreased sexual inhibitions in a world where such personal concerns already are close to nonexistent. Long a spring break staple, wet T-Shirt contests are relatively prudish compared to what's happening today on the beaches and in the clubs. Stripping and dancing contests—along with all sorts of games forcing participants to simulate sex—are common fare. In Mardis Gras fashion, young women readily flash their breasts in exchange for beads. But these public displays are only the start. Couples and groups engage in a variety of more intimate sexual behaviors, including intercourse and oral sex. The study done by that southern university found that 42 percent of guys and 22 percent of girls fooled around with someone they met during spring break. My guess is that those figures grossly underestimate the amount of spring break sexual activity.

> It's a marketer's bonanza.
> Sadly, what's given away more than anything else
> is the notion that "things bring happiness."

Of particular concern are the forced sexual encounters, or "date rapes," that take place as guys take advantage of drunken women or girls who have been unknowingly drugged with tasteless and odorless date rape drugs. Even those who choose not to drink can fall victim to the dangerous behaviors of those who choose to drink and drive.

Fourth, spring break is a time ripe for students to become victims of crime, including those just mentioned. Along with a multitude of travel scams, theft and destructive behavior are rampant. Not only are hotel rooms robbed, they're often trashed or destroyed by occupants who show little or no respect for property.

Finally, spring break is a time for marketers to line up their sights on young attendees. Capturing the heart of a young person and gaining their loyalty to a particular brand or product leads numerous companies to set up shop on streets and beaches or in clubs. College and high school students are preparing to make money and they want to make lots of it. In our material-oriented culture, they're also deciding where they're going to spend those hard-earned dollars. Everything from alcohol to clothing to cigarettes to credit cards to food to music is advertised and given away during spring break. It's a marketer's bonanza. Sadly, what's given away more than anything else is the notion that "things bring happiness."

So how should we respond to our kids' growing affinity to participate in this world of pleasure? First, we need to realize that education about the dangers of spring break and senior week should begin at a young age. And rather than doing nothing more than pronouncing a negative judgment—"it's bad"—on spring break, we should bring the light of God's Word to bear on those aspects that are wrong and immoral. We should teach and model a high regard for God's Word and our responsibility to engage in grateful obedience to the one who gave his Son for our salvation.

We should also teach and model a biblical sexual ethic. We should discuss and exemplify a lifestyle of freedom from alcohol dependence and abuse. Building a strong foundation is the best way to pave the way for our kids to choose an alternative spring break activity, or alternative activities while on spring break.

Second, we should continue to warn our kids who choose to go on spring break of the dangers—both moral and physical—they will encounter. The fact is that our young adult children are on their own and making their own decisions. Some will choose not to go. Others will. If our relationships with them are healthy, respectful, and loving, they will value our opinions highly. Hopefully, they will choose to avoid putting themselves in situations where compromise might come easily. Some may even be strong enough to attend and resist falling into temptation. For those who choose to go, we must exercise our parental

Opie Doesn't Live Here Anymore

rights and responsibilities, acting out of love by warning and admonishing where necessary.

Third, we must pray for our kids, not only during the decision-making process, but also after their decision has been made. If they've decided to go, you can be sure they'll face many difficult decisions over the duration of their trip. In my case, I always boldly pray that my kids will be absolutely miserable if they choose to walk a path outside of God's will and absolutes.

Fourth, we must always remind our believing children of the need to integrate their faith into all of life. Yes, there are rules. With the help of the Holy Spirit, they can be consistent. God grieves over our inconsistency. Challenge them to prayerfully seek God's will and live with a consistent faith that directs their every thought, word, and deed.

> I always boldly pray that my kids will be absolutely miserable if they choose to walk a path outside of God's will and absolutes.

And finally, challenge them to "run the race" by throwing off everything that will hold them back and the sin that so easily can wrap around their feet to trip them up (Hebrews 12:1). Whether it's sexual immorality, drunkenness, selfishness, or materialism, our kids need to learn how to recognize and avoid the traps.

Last year, I logged onto a Web site advertising a spring break vacation package. It billed itself as "the ultimate site for college students who . . . just can't stop thinking about spring break all year long!!" The site goes on to advertise every college student's "ultimate dream vacation." What's it like? According to the site it's "an escape from reality. . . . admittedly filled with beaches, endless nights of music, partying, sex, and anything but textbooks!"

For a college or high school student, that's very appealing. How sad. Let's pray that our kids would desire to make good and godly decisions—choices that will lead them to tap into the wonderful reality of life lived to the glory of God. That, and only that, is the ultimate!

There's a Virus in the Air

Youthculture@today; June 2003

On Thursday morning, April 24, I was sitting in my office screening rap star Eminem's popular biopic, *8 Mile*. About the time I was halfway through the film, a coworker, Cliff, ran into the room and told me to turn on the television. There had been another school shooting. The only difference this time was that it was our local media outlets covering an incident right here in our own part of the world. Even though all the facts weren't known, reporters were telling viewers that a fourteen-year-old middle school student had shot and killed a much-loved and highly respected principal, and then turned the gun on himself.

When the regular television coverage resumed, I turned off the TV, spun around in my chair, and shut down the DVD player in my computer. Eminem's movie could wait until another day. I picked up my note tablet—the one I had been filling with comments and observations while watching the film—and looked at the last words I had scribbled before being interrupted: "The film proposes and models a method of conflict resolution. That method is violence."

I didn't know the facts of the Red Lion school shooting outside of what I'd heard in the news. I knew nothing at all—nor would I speculate—about the personal life and specific motivation of the young man who pulled the trigger. In fact, I hurt deeply for his family and kept them in my prayers. All I knew was that two people were dead, their families were in great pain, hundreds of school children lost a good chunk of their innocence, and a community began asking the difficult and confusing "Why?" and "How?" questions.

I also knew that before choosing his tragic end, that young student had spent his brief fourteen years living in a culture that glorifies violence. I can say that with certainty because my four kids are growing up in the same world. It's the reality all our children face.

> **Before choosing his tragic end, that young student had spent his brief fourteen years living in a culture that glorifies violence.**

The story of fifteen-year-old Kip Kinkel's May 1998 shooting rampage offers compelling evidence of our culture's violent bent and collective loss of innocence. After killing his parents, he killed two of his Springfield, Oregon, classmates and wounded more than twenty others. Kids who knew Kinkel had taken in stride his frequent mentions of his desire to shoot cats, blow up cows, build bombs, kill people, and blow up the world. One journalist even discovered that students in Kinkel's literature class laughed when he read them a journal entry about his plans to "kill everybody." During investigations after the shooting, Kinkel's teachers said they hadn't reacted with alarm since a lot of kids in the school and around the country were saying the same things.

How have we gotten to the place where "killing talk" and behavior among our kids has become so commonplace that it doesn't even shake us anymore? Perhaps it's because a combination of cultural forces have merged so strongly to create a breeding ground for this virus of violence that we don't even know we've contracted it until it takes lives close to home.

> How have we gotten to the place where "killing talk" and behavior among our kids has become so commonplace that it doesn't even shake us anymore?

When I was asked to go to Littleton, Colorado, four years ago last April, my interactions with a community reeling from the Columbine shootings left me with the realization that, if it were at all possible, they would have given anything to turn back the clock to address and undo the combination of forces that led two boys named Klebold and Harris to kill.

While I was in Littleton, I heard lots of folks bemoan the fact that it was "too late." Too late to spend time loving those kids through the impressionable and life-shaping years of childhood and adolescence. Too late to teach them that there are such things as right and wrong. Too late to teach them that respect and responsibility are foundational to a strong and healthy society. Too late to eliminate from their media diet the films, TV shows, and music that glorify violence. Too late to encourage a student population that can so easily destroy kids through harassment and ridicule to see and treat each of their peers as a human being created in the image of God, worthy of respect. Too late to teach them that violence is not the way to solve problems. Too late to teach them what it means to follow the words of the psalmist: "Turn from evil and do good; seek peace and pursue it" (Psalm 34:14).

The most recent school shooting reminds us that we can't sit idly by and watch as the virus of violence infects more and more young hearts and minds. It's time to put forth a concerted effort to work at recovering our children's lost innocence, and to work at replacing a collective heart that too often sees violence as a solution with a heart that has a clear sense of right and wrong.

It's a complex problem that doesn't have easy answers. But don't let that lead you into the trap of thinking it's "too late." It's not too late to teach our own kids right from wrong.

One step in that direction is to turn off the media and video game violence in our homes. Fill that time with love, involvement, and attention. We're mistaken if we think our children are being entertained and not educated by what they see.

> **Turn off the media and video game violence in our homes. Fill that time with love, involvement, and attention.**

It's not too late to challenge other parents to face the nasty reality of the role that media violence plays in the lives of their kids. And it's not too late to identify and reach out to those children and teens who aren't being raised in homes where involved parenting is a priority. They are sitting ducks waiting to be swept away by the prevailing winds of cultural attitudes. We must spend time with them, love them, nurture their faith, and point them in the right direction through the power of relationships and example.

Our words and example should ooze the truths Jesus spoke in the Sermon on the Mount (Matthew 5–7). First, "Blessed are the peacemakers, for they will be called sons of God." As followers of Christ, we should never seek nor be responsible for conflict. Instead, we should seek *shalom*, that condition of freedom from both internal and external strife. Likewise, our prayer and purpose for our children should be to see them spared from the internal strife that so frequently yields a harvest of external violence. Second, "Do not resist an evil person." This negative command makes it clear that God calls us to passive nonretaliation. And finally, "Love your enemies." In this positive command, Christ calls his followers to actively love and pray for their persecutors.

In this positive command, Christ calls his followers to actively love and pray for their persecutors.

I wonder how one twenty-one-year-old's life might be different if someone had entered his life, living and telling these truths. I recently read the disturbing story of this unnamed young man from British Columbia. When he was only seventeen, he had a sexual relationship with his twenty-nine-year-old, married school teacher. At the time of the affair, the court ordered a publication ban on the young man's name in order to protect his identity. Several weeks ago, he asked the court to lift the ban so that he can pursue a career in rap music built on the publicity

Opie Doesn't Live Here Anymore

from his case. He's made a gangsta rap CD filled with violence, profanity, boasts about seducing his teacher, and references to his hate of the Royal Canadian Mounted Police. In an effort to sell the CD—titled *Teacher's Scandal*—he's promoting his image as "a bada--" and has depicted himself on the CD cover posing with a sawed-off shotgun and a chainsaw. Sadly, he's caught the virus. Even more distressing, he's actively promoting its spread.

The cost of the virus of violence has been hearts, minds, and lives. The cure for the virus of violence and the prescription for the recovery of innocence lie in diligent commitment to teaching and modeling God's unchanging standards of ethical behavior, diligent parenting, diligent prayer, and diligent involvement in the lives of children and teens.

What part in spreading the cure will you and I choose to play?

CONFUSION OR CLARITY?
YOUTH CULTURE AT THE CROSSROADS

Youthculture@today; June 2002

He survives a plane crash into the sea and, after weathering four years on an uninhabited island, Chuck Noland is rescued and brought back to civilization. Noland—played brilliantly by Tom Hanks in the film *Cast Away*—represents each of us and the options we face on the way to choosing what we value in our quest for meaning and purpose in life.

In the film's moving final scene, Noland— a man changed by four years of forced isolation and introspection—stands at the middle of a quiet and desolate intersection on the stark Texas plains. Not sure which direction to take, the movie closes as he surveys his four options, each of which stretches straight to a seemingly endless and unknown horizon.

On a recent trip to downtown Manhattan, I gathered some sense of what it must be like to be a teen standing at the noisy and crowded crossroads of adolescence in today's youth culture. It was five o'clock in the afternoon—the peak of rush hour—on a rainy Tuesday afternoon. I was walking through Times Square with some friends. My senses were overloaded by activity happening in every direction. A 360-degree spin filled my field of vision—up, down, and side-to-side—with people, cars, and advertisements. The smells of hot dogs and soft pretzels were making me hungry. I stopped and satisfied my taste buds. I was surrounded by the sounds of hustle and bustle, everything from taxi horns to barking street vendors to loud music pumped onto the street from storefronts. Even my sense of touch came into play as I got pushed, shoved, and bumped in the rushing river of people moving to and from who knows where. One of my friends, Mike, turned to me and said, "This is amazing, isn't it? It's known as the crossroads of the world!" I could only think, *If I didn't already know where I was heading, how would I know where to go?*

Adolescence is a period of life spent at the crossroads. It's a time marked by overwhelming change, numerous questions, and a search for answers. But the crossroads where our youth stand is anything but quiet and desolate. Not sure which direction to take, our children and teens are presented with an abundance of confusing options. The noise can be deafening. Perhaps the signposts they choose to follow are the ones that are the most attractive,

Opie Doesn't Live Here Anymore

loud, and convincing in response to their unspoken teenage cry of "Show me the way!"

As I look at the choices, pressures, and challenges facing kids in today's youth culture, there are some signposts that seem to be attracting more attention than others. No matter where our kids position themselves at the crossroads, these signs fill their field of vision and overload their senses with pointed and powerful persuasion, saying "This is the way!"

> **Not sure which direction to take, our children and teens are presented with an abundance of confusing options. The noise can be deafening.**

If we care about kids, where they are and where they're headed, we've got to look at the signposts that are catching their attention and leading them along in life. By looking at the most popular and powerful signposts, we can gain insight into our children's needs and questions, as well as the sense of urgency and diligence needed to provide them with proper direction. In this way they can also serve as signposts for us, pointing the way to a land of crisis that is in desperate need of spiritual relief aid. As I stand with kids at the crossroads, here are three troubling signposts—all getting bigger, increasingly attractive, and more effective by the minute—that I see grabbing their attention.

There is the signpost of anything and everything sexual. This signpost points away from the freedom and joy of experiencing God's wonderful gift of sexuality within the lifelong covenant and commitment of marriage. That's God's intended best! Instead, it points to a place where kids are encouraged and expected to indulge their sexuality wherever, however, whenever, and with whomever.

On my trip to Times Square I saw evidence of this attitude when I looked up at one of those "so big you can't miss it" billboards hanging on the side of a building over the crowd. There was contemporary poster girl Pamela Anderson totally naked, lying on the front of a huge basketball shoe. A sentence packed with sexual innuendo completes the ad: "IT JUST FEELS BIGGER." The billboard had become an accepted and even normal feature of the landscape at the "world's crossroads." If our culture's acceptance of that visual message isn't convincing enough, then mark your calendar to check out MTV's dose of special spring break programming that will air next spring. Once you watch you'll agree: kids have followed this signpost.

Then there is the signpost of postmodern relativism. While the relativistic signpost has been sitting at the crossroads for a long time, its growing influence has led to a larger following. It points to an amoral place where the thread of commonly held standards that once ran through the tapestry of our culture has been removed from the fabric. Instead, what's left is "I have my truth and you have yours." Neither one is right for anyone else unless, of course, he or she chooses that "truth" as their own at that given point in time.

And while tolerance of varying viewpoints is celebrated as a virtue, that virtue is quickly giving way to celebrating varying viewpoints alone. I kept my eye on the "pond" of today's youth culture when Rosie O'Donnell—a favorite among children and teens—outed herself earlier this year. There wasn't a ripple of negative or even concerned response in that pond. After all, "Rosie can do whatever Rosie wants to do."

I've also watched as MTV's reality peek into the twisted home life of burned-out rocker Ozzy Osbourne's family has gripped young viewers, vaulting *The Osbournes* into television history as the most popular show ever on MTV and the most popular show on cable at this moment in time. Each episode features the family's profanity-filled conversations and rantings. Poor Ozzy is so fried by his lifestyle of rocker excess that he struggles to finish a sentence, complete a thought, and lift a glass to his mouth with his shaky hands. Rarely, if ever, does the show warrant adjectives of young audience response such as "sad," "sorry," "depressing," or "wrong." Instead, our culture laughs collectively because "it's hilarious." After all, who's to say that there's anything wrong with the Osbournes and the way they've chosen to live their lives? I think you'll agree—our kids have followed this relativistic signpost.

> Instead, our culture laughs collectively because "it's hilarious." After all, who's to say that there's anything wrong with the Osbournes and the way they've chosen to live their lives?

And there is the signpost of the deconstructed God. The great news is that youth culture is wearing spirituality on its sleeve. It's exciting to know that suddenly it's OK to talk, sing, and write about God. But the spoken-, sung-, and written-about god is not necessarily the God who has revealed himself in his written Word, the Bible, and in the incarnate Word, Jesus Christ. Instead, today's gods are created in the image and personal preference of everyone who speaks, sings, and writes.

In his best-selling book, *Conversations with God for Teens*, Neale Donald Walsch channels "god" by asking "god" the questions teens would love to ask "god." He explains his methodology to his readers this way: "Now it might sound good if I said that I ponder my questions for hours, meditating and praying and remaining in the stillness until I am brought to enlightenment and tremble with the energy flowing through my fingertips. But the truth is, I put down the first thing that comes to my head."[10] The fruit of this methodology is a book full of answers for kids needing a signpost—answers that can be reduced to this axiom: "I (God) say that you can do whatever you want to do." This new "god" looks and sounds nothing like the God who was, is, and always will be. Walsch's is a god who tells teens: "Right and wrong do not exist as absolutes, but only as momentary assessments of What Works and What Doesn't Work. You make these assessments yourself, as individuals and as a society, given what you are wishing to experience and how you see yourself in relationship to everything else that is."[11] It's frightening to ponder, but I think you'll agree—kids have followed this signpost.

> ## So what do we do? Sit back and complain? Do we try to silence the signposts we don't like by taking an ax to their bases?

So what do we do? Sit back and complain? Do we try to silence the signposts we don't like by taking an ax to their bases? Perhaps the best approach is illustrated by something else I saw on that rainy, Times Square Tuesday back in March. As we walked down the sidewalk I noticed a group of people—mostly young, but some old—set apart from the rest of the crowd by their jackets. It looked like there were about thirty of them, all wearing bright yellow windbreakers. They stood out like sore thumbs. The logo and text printed on the backs of their matching jackets identified them as a high school group from New Mexico. They were spending the afternoon visiting the crossroads of the world. The barrage of sights, sounds, and "signposts" was peppering them from every direction.

As we got closer, it was obvious the group's adult chaperones had strategically placed themselves at the front, rear, and sides of the group. Like a group of border collies, they kept the teens herded together and moving to their intended destination. As I passed, I asked the chaperone bringing up the rear about his group and their trip. Then, before I walked on, I remarked, "I think the yellow jackets are a brilliant idea." His response: "They sure are! This way we can keep our eyes on them and they can keep their eyes on us. We know right where they are and they can see us. We don't want to lose any kids in a place like this." Perhaps our role—as parents, youth workers, and the church in the twenty-first century—is to serve as border collies of sorts.

It's easy for kids to get lost in the negative aspects of today's youth culture. They're standing at the crossroads and deciding which way to go. As the people of God, we've got to keep our eyes on them. We need to know right where they are. We must be aware of the signposts they're tempted to follow.

But there is an even larger responsibility as well. In his classic book on discipleship, *The Fight*, Dr. John White reminds us of our need to be more than mere border collies. Instead, we must become living signposts ourselves. "A signpost points to a destination," White writes. "It matters little whether the signpost is pretty or ugly, old or new. It helps if the lettering is bold and clear. But the essential features are that it must point in the right direction and be clear about what it is pointing to."[12]

The kids you and I know—what signs do they see? Which direction are we pointing them to?

The kids you and I know—what signs do they see? Which direction are we pointing them to? Is it to the wide and well-traveled road that leads to destruction? Or down the narrow road that leads to life?

Will we serve as signposts for truth—markers so large and convincing that we eclipse the signposts already there?

Opie Doesn't Live Here Anymore

EMBRACING THE COLLISION

*Since my youth, O God, you have taught me, and to this day
I declare your marvelous deeds. Even when I am old and
gray, do not forsake me, O God, till I declare your power
to the next generation, your might to all who are to come.*
(Psalm 71:17, 18)

*When the foundations are being destroyed, what can the
righteous do? The Lord is in his holy temple; the Lord is on
his heavenly throne.* (Psalm 11:3, 4)

*Trust in the Lord with all your heart and lean not on your
own understanding; in all your ways acknowledge him, and
he will make your paths straight.* (Proverbs 3:5, 6)

1. WHAT IS YOUR REACTION TO MY FATHER'S REMARK,
"I'm glad I'm not raising kids in today's world"? How
has the world changed in the last fifty years? How has it
remained the same?

2. "THE SCRIPTURES ARE CLEAR: GOD IS NOT CONCERNED WITH OUTWARD APPEARANCE. Rather, God is concerned with our hearts." Why is this so difficult for our kids—and for us—to grasp?

3. SOMETIMES WE ASSUME WE CAN SOMEHOW MAKE OUR KIDS IMMUNE TO THE INFLUENCE OF CULTURE by shielding them from that same culture. Why is this a naive approach?

4. WHAT IS MEANT BY LIVING A LIFE OF "dis-integrated" faith?

5. WHY DO SO MANY KIDS FAIL TO INTEGRATE THEIR FAITH INTO ALL AREAS OF LIFE? What can we do to help them integrate their faith in a much stronger way?

Opie Doesn't Live Here Anymore

ON LOVE AND LIFE

I LOVE YOU.

I sometimes wonder how many billions of times those three small words have been uttered without knowledge of their true meaning. I spent a good part of my own life believing that love was a feeling. Consequently, I've made the mistake of thinking that the wonderful, yet temporary, feeling of infatuation was love. And sometimes "love" fizzled out faster than it had fired up in the first place.

And then there are the mistaken expectations I make about my life. I fall into the trap of thinking life is meant to be painless and trouble-free. Then, when difficulty shows up at the front door, forcing its way into my life, I do anything to squash it so I can go back to easy living.

My skewed perspective and expectations regarding love and life were fed by a combination of immaturity, youthful idealism, and growing up in the comfort of a consumer culture that consistently promised peace for a price. But by God's grace, the lies I believed were shattered by the realities of life, and by seeing those realities through the corrective lenses of a biblical worldview.

Even though I'm still learning—most of the time the hard way—I no longer look at love and life the way I once did. Being a son, husband, father, friend, and follower of Christ has changed the way I define and live out love. Feelings come and go; living life guided by emotions is a dangerous, even deadly way to exist. Instead, I've come to understand that love is commitment, specifically the selfless commitment that looks and longs for absolutely nothing in return.

And I've learned that to love—truly love—is hard work. I'm sure I've done a good job convincing those closest to

Opie Doesn't Live Here Anymore

me of the same thing. I don't think I'm easy to love. Yet I'm humbled by receiving human love.

I'm humbled most of all, however, by the overflow of love that hits me on all sides from the one who chose to rescue and adopt me. Ultimately, that's what has shaped my growing understanding and experience of love and life. What follows are some of my thoughts as I strive to make God the model I look to for loving—and living.

I Love You 12

Youthculture@today; September 2001

I never thought this day would arrive. Back in December 1983, the fall of 2001 was light-years away. But in hindsight, it went as quickly as an overnight. It's as if I fell asleep holding my newborn first child in my arms, and then I woke up, looked down at her, and found myself staring in disbelief at a young woman. I remember older, more experienced parents warning me it would happen this way, but I didn't believe them at the time. I guess they were right.

Just about the time you'll be reading these words, our seventeen-year-old daughter, Caitlin, will be starting her senior year in high school. Over the next few months she'll turn eighteen, decide where she wants to attend college next fall, and graduate from high school. God willing—and if everything goes as planned—she'll also take a one-way ride in a car loaded down with clothes, boxes, bags, and anything else she can cram in. Lisa and I will help her lug all that stuff into a dorm room, hug her, issue more instructions than she'll want to hear (as usual!), tell her we love her, say a tearful good-bye, and then head home as Caitlin starts the next phase of her life.

> Lisa and I will help her lug all that stuff into a dorm room, hug her, issue more instructions than she'll want to hear (as usual!), tell her we love her, and say a tearful good-bye.

I've written a letter to Caitlin that I've decided to share with you. It doesn't include everything I want to say to her as she starts her last year of high school. But it does communicate my prayers and desires for her as her father and as one who watches the culture in which she lives every day. To be honest, my words are not written to Caitlin alone—they're for me as well. Perhaps you'll find them challenging too.

Fall 2001

Dear Caitlin,

Lately I've found myself consumed with a confusing mix of emotions as I think about this, your last year of high school. My guess is that this will be a year of many "lasts" for you—your last year at home, your last prom, your last year playing high school hockey and soccer, your last year of math (hooray!!), and more. I know these are things you've been thinking about too.

The hardest part for me has been thinking about the new kind of good-bye I'm going to have to learn to say when Mom and I drop you off at school next fall. That will be an exciting time of new beginnings for you, and it will be one of those parent/child conversations I'm sure none of us will ever forget.

As I make a deliberate effort to enjoy your senior year with you while learning to let go of my oldest child for the first time, I've found myself thinking back over the years to the many wonderful conversations and times we've spent together. Those memories always start with December 1, 1983, and the moment I held you for the first time.

That moment seems like yesterday to me. You were maybe five to ten seconds old when Dr. Edwards put you into my arms. I had the privilege of excitedly telling your mother, "Lisa, it's a little girl! And she's beautiful!" Then I said some words that were probably pretty frightening to everyone in the room—"She looks just like me!" That was the first time you heard my voice. Shortly after that—not surprisingly—you started to really cry. Sorry to have done that to you! Fortunately for you and the rest of the world, God's shown his favor to you by allowing you to grow up to look like your mother!

Since that most incredible of days, you've heard my voice over and over and over again. I hope you agree that most of our conversations have been good ones. Some we probably both regret. But while our many memorable conversations are too numerous to recount in this letter, there's one favorite of mine that we had too many times to count. When I think about it, it always makes me smile. Do you remember the recurring conversation I'm talking about? I remember the first time we had it. You were little—maybe three or four—and I said to you, "Caitlin, I love you." You eagerly responded, "Daddy, I love you too." Then I asked, "How much do you love me?" You answered, "I love you 12!" I just assumed that was the highest number you knew at the time and it was your way of telling me you loved me as much as any little girl could. We had that conversation so many times when you were little. From time to time over the years we've stepped back and relived that interchange as you've continued to tell me that you love me "12."

> Then I asked, "How much do you love me?" You answered, "I love you 12!" I just assumed that was the highest number you knew at the time and it was your way of telling me you loved me as much as any little girl could.

As you've grown up, our conversations haven't always been as humorous or positive. We've disagreed, argued, and been frustrated with each other. That's normal. But, while I know you sometimes get tired of hearing my voice—all my little talks, instructions, and never-ending questions—you can nonetheless be sure you'll have to endure the same kind of adulthood that your grandfather has given to me! Yes, I'll continue to offer my advice regardless of whether or not you ask for it. Some call it "a father's privilege." I think it's something more like "a father's love." So once again, I want to show my love for you by passing on some words to a daughter who has brought me such great joy through her passion for life, sense of humor, creativity, and yes, even her impulsive spontaneity!

> **The world will encourage you to see yourself as number one. But don't be self-centered. You were made by God to be God-centered.**

Because that number, 12, was such a big part of your expression of deep love for me when you were little, I want to lovingly remind you of 12 character traits I hope and pray will be descriptive of who you become as you prepare to leave our house and move out into the world. Because of my deep love for you, I pray that these traits would be evident in your life—during your last year of high school and throughout your future. Each is a quality highly valued by God that is increasingly forgotten or frowned upon by many in our society and youth culture. Caitlin, if you prayerfully seek to live out these traits in today's world, you'll be fulfilling the purpose you were created for as a dearly loved child of God.

First and foremost, glorify God in everything you are and everything you do. Live for the one who died for you by turning to him as the guide and director of all your thoughts, all your feelings, and all your actions. The world will encourage you to see yourself as number one. But don't be self-centered. You were made by God to be God-centered. Praise and glorify God by how you live, how you study, how you play, how you converse, and how you relate.

Second, strive to be consistent in your faith. If you are looking for models of how to talk about following Christ while actually living by other priorities, there are plenty out there. In fact, the church is increasingly marked by "dis-integrated" Christians. Caitlin, ask God to help you look closely at your life each and every day. Ask him to expose those areas of your life where you must allow him to rule. Strive for a life of integration. Your faith should not be just one part of your life. Instead, it should guide, direct, permeate, and inform every area of your life.

> **Live a life marked by grace. I realize how much I've failed to live this way in my relationship with you.**

Third, be full of thanksgiving. Everything you have, are, and do is a gift from God. Don't think they come from you. Instead, realize that all the good gifts you experience are purely by the grace of God. And when you experience emotional, spiritual, or physical difficulty—and you will—be sure to thank God for those gifts as well. Why? Because he's given you those difficulties as part of the refining process. He's growing your faith. Gratefully recognize the source of your blessings.

Fourth, develop and use discernment. Your life will be full of choices, many of them difficult. Caitlin, the world *is encouraging you to make decisions based on what feels good to you at the moment. You're already surrounded by people who live that way. This will only get worse. Make all your decisions—what you listen to, what you watch, who you choose as close friends, who you marry, how you spend your time, what you do vocationally—on the basis of God's unchanging Word. Don't trust your changing feelings as a gauge to discover and do what seems right. Instead, study and follow God's Word so that you can choose to do what is right.*

Fifth, live a life marked by grace. I realize how much I've failed to live this way in my relationship with you. I'm learning that as your earthly father, I must relate to you with the same measure of grace my heavenly Father has given me. Grace is undeserved favor. Its greatest expression came in the gift of the life, death, and resurrection of Jesus on our behalf—something we could never earn or deserve. Caitlin, show that same grace to every person you encounter.

> I remember when you took a slow time in the mile run, when you could have easily finished at the front of the pack. Instead, you ran with a girl who struggled to even finish—encouraging her all the way across the finish line.

Sixth, continue to be a person of compassion. Mom and I have always been proud of you for the way you seem to go out of your way to love those who don't get too much love. I remember when you took a slow time in the mile run, when you could have easily finished at the front of the pack. Instead, you ran with a girl who struggled to even finish—

encouraging her all the way across the finish line. Jesus was a friend to the friendless. He was sympathetic, kind, and merciful. Do the same.

7. *Seventh, always show humility. Don't ever believe that your talents, gifts, abilities, successes, and achievements come from you. If anyone deserves a pat on the back for those things, it's not you. Don't ever allow yourself to be full of self-centered pride. Do you know those conversations I've had with Josh when we are watching a football game and someone does one of those "Aren't I great?!?" dances in the end zone after scoring a touchdown? I'll say the same thing to you that I've told him: Don't ever do that! Don't ever be puffed up by a false sense of your own self-importance.*

8. *Eighth, live a life marked by self-control. Rein yourself in and don't let the world set the agenda for how you live. The world will tell you how to live out your sexuality. The world will tell you how to view material things. The world will tell you how to treat other people. Sadly, the world will tell you that in these and all other areas you have the freedom to choose and use your own rules. But instead of living a life of excess, imitate Christ and live a life of discipline by striving to please God.*

9. *Ninth, always respect and obey authority. God is your king. He has established authorities in your life you are called to respect, honor, and obey, as long as they don't require you to do something in opposition to God's will. Yes, I know I've always reminded you that children are to obey their parents! Caitlin, continue to respect, honor, and obey your teachers, coaches, and all others in authority.*

10. *Tenth, be a woman marked by sexual purity. I've driven all you kids nuts on this one, but for good reason. You get one shot on this and one shot alone. Sadly, you get that*

one shot to follow God's will and design for his incredible gift of sexuality in a world that makes a joke out of God's sexual plan. Don't buy the lies that there are no rules. Stand firm on this, Caitlin, because there will be opportunity for compromise and resulting regret. Decide now to live what you know to be true—trust and believe that God has your best interest in mind and that he wants you to experience the joy of sexual fulfillment in the context of lifelong marital commitment. You won't regret it.

Eleventh, maintain a strong sense of modesty. We live in a society that has lost all respect for female modesty. In fact, the world around you will encourage you to let it all hang out. Caitlin, work to carefully, deliberately, and consciously honor God through what you say, how you act, and what you wear. Remember that in God's eyes—the only eyes you need to please—modesty, chastity, honor, and restraint are all virtues.

> Don't buy the lies that there are no rules. Stand firm on this, Caitlin, because there will be opportunity for compromise and resulting regret.

Finally, never cease being fully dependent on God. Solomon wrote these wise words: "Trust in the Lord with all your heart and lean not on your own understanding; in all your ways acknowledge him, and he will make your paths straight" (Proverbs 3:5, 6).

Caitlin, as you prepare to leave our house, my prayer is that you would continue to be beautiful, not only in an outward sense—but more importantly in terms of your character. My prayer is that as you grow in age and faith, you will be truly conformed into the image and likeness of

*Jesus Christ. Then every time I see you I can turn to your
mother and say, "Lisa, it's our little girl. And she's beautiful—
she looks just like her Father."*

I love you "12,"
Dad

I Love You Just the Way You Are

Youthculture@today; December 1997

I experienced pains of anticipatory agony the night before
my seventh-grade gym class assembled on the cinder
quarter-mile track for the annual mile run for time. I
remember praying two prayers as I lay fitfully awake on
that eve of aerobic despair: *God, please help me finish!* and
Please don't let me finish last! Both prayers were answered.

Unfortunately, I remember something else about that
day. After the run, I joined my peers in that all-too-
common junior high ritual that leaves many kids feeling
like a heap of trash: we laughed at the overweight and
out-of-breath kid who once again crossed the finish line
last and all alone.

> **I joined my peers in that all-too-common junior high ritual
> that leaves many kids feeling like a heap of trash:
> we laughed at the overweight and out-of-breath kid who
> once again crossed the finish line last and all alone.**

The early adolescent years are a combination of fast-
paced change and the confusion of wondering, *Am I
normal?* Add to this insecurity the desire to fit in and a
peer group that knows little or nothing about sensitivity

Opie Doesn't Live Here Anymore

and you've got a volatile mix. Do you remember what it was like to walk the junior high halls and feel as though every eye was focused on you and how you just didn't seem to measure up?

Sadly, it's still the same today. There are insecure kids who find themselves being labeled as popular, and there is the remaining insecure lot that gets crushed while serving as stepping-stones for those who are building themselves up by putting others down.

> Thin is not only in, it's highly desirable. Consequently, many kids are spending more time in front of the mirror, or more time lying awake anticipating another day of nasty junior high ridicule, or both.

However, the standards of today's acceptance game have been raised. The emphasis on physical beauty and body shape established by media icons have left changing girls and boys wondering, *Will I ever be, or look, good enough for somebody to love?* Thin is not only in, it's highly desirable. Consequently, many kids are spending more time in front of the mirror, or more time lying awake anticipating another day of nasty junior high ridicule, or both.

I read a news story about a twelve-year-old boy—I'll use only his first name, Sammy—who had one of those nights back in August 1996. With the first day of school scheduled for the next morning, this outstanding student from a solid, loving family had gone to bed after praying with his father and two young brothers. The next day, before anyone else was awake, Sammy took a flashlight, rope, and step stool into the backyard. Later, his father found Sammy's lifeless body hanging from a tree.

Sammy was frightened about the teasing he would have to put up with—and pained by what he had already endured—because his 5' 4" body carried 174 pounds. The pain of death became more bearable than the pain of ridicule. The pressure was just too much.

We can learn many lessons from Sammy. First, we must constantly remind our kids of their uniqueness as God's handiwork, knitted together and formed according to his purpose and plan. No matter how much worldly standards change, their heavenly Father continues to see each one as beautiful.

Of course, transferring this truth from mere words to reality requires a second step: We must point out the appearance lies of the world to our children and emphasize their standing in God's eyes by showering them with time, love, acceptance, and affection.

This battle with our culture's horribly skewed standards doesn't look to get easier anytime soon. But we do know that junior high kids who are confident in themselves and sensitive to others typically have something special happening in their relationships with dad and mom.

> **We must point out the appearance lies of the world to our children and emphasize their standing in God's eyes.**

Several times a week I run at our local school track. Recently, I've shared the track with a number of physical education students as they run the mile for time. (Poor kids!) During one recent jog I watched as the teacher blew his whistle, signaling the run's start. Naturally, the most

Opie Doesn't Live Here Anymore

athletic members of the class took off at a fast pace. The rest of the class lagged behind, but at least kept moving ahead.

> **Four laps together . . . start to finish.**
> **One person was saved from humiliation.**
> **The other—well, her parents should be proud.**

Then I watched in wonder as a beautiful sight unfolded. There on the track, far behind the pack and even farther behind the athletes, walked two figures side by side. One was a girl—terribly overweight. For her, running a mile was probably impossible. But walking next to her, voicing words of encouragement, was a slender and athletic-looking peer who looked as if she could have run well and perhaps even finished first.

Four laps together . . . start to finish. One person was saved from humiliation. The other—well, her parents should be proud.

I was reminded of the simple command of Jesus: "Love one another as I have loved you." I'm in the midst of watching two of my own children struggle with those junior high pressures and expectations. I'm convinced that living out these words of Jesus at home is one of the best gifts we can give our young adolescents.

HEARING THE CRY FOR COMPASSION

Youthculture@today; April 1999

> *Editor's note: This article was written two weeks before the fatal school shootings at Columbine High School in Littleton, Colorado, in April 1999. Keep those events in mind as you read.*

Yesterday was a bad day for our fifteen-year-old daughter, Caitlin. Lisa could see it on her face as soon as Caitlin climbed into the car after soccer practice. Through her tears, Caitlin explained that a student at her school had ended his life the night before.

Caitlin didn't know Chris personally, but she knew who he was. As we listened to Caitlin recount what little she knew about his life, it became increasingly obvious why a young man like Chris might choose the ugliness of self-inflicted death as more attractive than a hopeless life. Eighteen years old, Chris had struggled with academics; he was still in the tenth grade. He was overweight. Kids picked on him all the time. Caitlin commented on how she would see him walking down the hall between classes, his head always hung low. In the cafeteria she would see him eating alone. Kids say that on the day he died, he had been picked on particularly hard. She also knew that his life ended as he hung from the end of a rope.

> **Could it be that we ignore the cries for mercy because getting involved would require us to invest more of ourselves than we're willing to give?**

While Caitlin and her friends had never picked on Chris, I'm sure they were all thinking about what they might have done differently if they could have somehow rewound the clock by a week or two. Hindsight makes us do that following a tragedy. Maybe they would have talked to Chris in the hall. Perhaps they would have sat with him at lunch. But the ugly reality is that, for Chris, and so many other kids, their cries go unheard until after they've stopped. By then it's too late to give an answer.

Opie Doesn't Live Here Anymore

Why is it that we fail to hear the cries of the hopeless and hurting outcasts coming from so many corners of today's youth culture? Is it that we're too busy? Is it that we don't care? Could it be that we ignore the cries for mercy because getting involved would require us to invest more of ourselves than we're willing to give?

> **But then, backed into a corner, the inquisitor knew that he did not love in this way. Maybe he was just too busy, or didn't care. Maybe he didn't want to get involved.**

Jesus addressed this issue. A religious man who saw himself as wholeheartedly devoted to God once tested Jesus with this question: "What do I need to do to get eternal life?" Jesus responded with a question: "What's written in God's law? How do you interpret it?" The man answered, "That you love the Lord your God with all your passion and prayer and muscle and intelligence—and that you love your neighbor as well as you do yourself" (Luke 10:25-27, *The Message*). Jesus affirmed the man's answer. Basically, he told him: "Do it—keep on doing it—and you'll live."

But then, backed into a corner, the inquisitor knew that he did not love in this way. Maybe he was just too busy, or didn't care. Maybe he didn't want to get involved. Looking for a way out, he asked Jesus to define "neighbor," hoping to prove that not all people—especially those he did not like or have time for—qualified as "neighbors."

Jesus proceeded to tell a story that most of us have heard many times. It's about a Jewish man who is beaten, robbed, and left for dead on the side of the road. A religious man—a priest—comes by and, rather than stopping to help, passes by on the other side. The wounded man's cries for mercy go unanswered. Another religious man— a Levite—comes along, sees the hurting and hopeless traveler, but passes by as well. A third man walks by. He's a Samaritan, the least likely of the three at that time in history to reach out and help a Jew.

Yet this Samaritan hears the cries, takes pity on the dying man, and meets his needs. He painstakingly bandages his wounds. He lifts the man onto his own donkey and walks him to an inn where he can be made comfortable and find rest. And the Samaritan provides for the beaten man's long-term welfare by paying for his rehabilitation.

> **The roadside of today's youth culture is littered with bruised and battered kids—outcasts crying out for a rescuer.**

Jesus ended the story by asking these questions: "What do you think? Which of the three became a neighbor to the man attacked by robbers?" The man could give only one answer: "The one who treated him kindly" (Luke 10:36, 37, *The Message*).

Jesus then looked at his questioner—in fact, at all of us—and responded, "Go and do"—go and keep on doing—"the same" (Luke 10:37, *The Message*). We are called to exhibit the divine compassion of Christ at the sight of deep human need.

The roadside of today's youth culture is littered with bruised and battered kids—outcasts crying out for a rescuer. The same road is traveled by too many people claiming to be followers of Christ who never stop to help at the sight of deep pain, anger, and human need.

Opie Doesn't Live Here Anymore

Perhaps we should approach today's spiritually bruised and battered children and teens by praying the same prayer a man named Bob Pierce once offered as he looked around at a physically hungry world: *Let my heart be broken by the things that break the heart of God.* When God answered his prayer, Pierce couldn't help but respond to what he saw. That prayer yielded World Vision, a relief organization that has answered the physical and spiritual cries of thousands of children around the world.

If our prayers are sincere, I believe they will yield the Christ-like compassion and pity that the outcasts left by the side of the road by today's youth culture so badly need to see. Only God can develop those types of responses in us, emotions of deep sympathy working themselves out in a complete willingness to use all the time, means, strength, and life at our disposal to act on behalf of another.

Shortly after 3 AM on March 13, 1964, after getting off work, a twenty-eight-year-old New Yorker named Kitty Genovese was walking the short distance left from her car to her apartment. She never made it. Genovese was attacked—beaten, assaulted, stabbed, and raped. She cried and screamed for help until she was hoarse. Her attacker left her for dead. A few minutes later, he came back and attacked her again. She screamed for help. Less than a half-hour after he first attacked her, he came back and assaulted her a third time. Genovese screamed again. Then the man walked away. Medical personnel found her in a Queens alleyway just yards from the safety of her apartment, but it was too late. Kitty Genovese died; the entire attack was estimated to have taken about thirty-two minutes.

What makes this story particularly appalling is that as Genovese screamed, cried, and lay dying, numerous people got out of bed and watched from their windows. No one came to help. No one called for help. When it was done and her cries had stopped, they walked away from their windows, turned out the lights, and went back to sleep.

Eventually, police identified and captured her attacker, a man named Winston Moseley. Their search of the neighborhood for witnesses led to the grim discovery that thirty-eight people had watched at least some part of the attack—and done nothing. During Moseley's trial the witnesses were asked why they didn't help Genovese. Their collective answer: "We didn't want to get involved." When Moseley took the stand, he was asked why he kept coming back to attack Genovese when he could see all those people watching from their windows. He responded, "I knew they wouldn't do anything—they never do."

Could the same be said of the church today?

In her best-selling book *Traveling Mercies*, author Anne Lamott chronicles her unusual journey to faith. I was in the middle of reading Lamott's book on the day Chris was found dangling from a rope. Lamott's confusing life echoes the little bit I've heard about Chris. There was one big difference: while Lamott—a self-described outcast—lay hopeless and dying on the side of the road, a small group of people from a church came upon her and stopped to help. She writes: "When I was at the end of my rope, the people at St. Andrews tied a knot in it for me and helped me hold on. The church became my home in the old meaning of *home*—that it's where, when you show

Opie Doesn't Live Here Anymore

up, they have to let you in. They let me in. They even said, 'You come back now.'"[1]

Jesus said, "Go and keep on doing the same."

BAD MAKES CHRISTMAS GOOD

Blog; December 22, 2005

For the last couple of weeks I've been going through my annual ritual of trying to recapture that Christmas holiday spirit that always filled me with an eager and expectant emotional high when I was a kid. Back then, the days leading up to the big morning dragged on, and nothing went as slow as that close-to-sleepless night before Christmas. We had our rituals—eat lots of my aunt's cookies, get dressed up for church, hold a candle while singing "Silent Night" at the end of the service (the pyromaniac in me loved that one!), come home to eat more of my aunt's cookies and drink some nonalcoholic eggnog (fresh from the cardboard carton my mom had picked up at the local 7-Eleven), leave some of my aunt's cookies out for the man in red—and then, finally, go to bed.

Time never drags that slow for me anymore. Wasn't it just summer? Now I have to work to get into the spirit of Christmas past. Part of this year's work has included keeping my car radio tuned to the station that's playing Christmas music around the clock. Well, some of it is Christmas music. I've been listening a bit harder this year. I can hum along to most of the tunes without even thinking about them. But when I listen I'm sometimes shocked by what I hear . . . and have heard for years. I've realized this year, like never before, that most of the songs are about yearning for connections, personal peace, good feelings, and that same holiday spirit I search for.

It's ironic, though, that songs occasioned by the earth-shattering historical event that enables connections, personal peace, and the real spirit of the holiday don't say much about that historical event at all. And the emptiness continues. This Christmas, there will be a lot of people dealing with lots of garbage—you know, the type that we hear "makes the holidays difficult" for so many. Death, loss, illness, hurricanes, earthquakes, tsunamis, and more.

I'm thinking about Christmas a bit differently myself because of the garbage that's entered my own life. The guy who used to string the lights, set up the tree, build the train platform, and preach the gospel message at our church every year won't be at home for Christmas. This time last year he was in the pulpit. This year he's lying in a nursing home bed. At times, I've been tempted to scream "NOT FAIR!" But then I remember . . . it was *me* who made the world this way. Yeah, it's bad. Thanks to my actions and your actions, we should expect nothing less than an endless string of garbage.

> The guy who used to string the lights, set up the tree, build the train platform, and preach the gospel message at our church every year won't be at home for Christmas . . . This year he's lying in a nursing home bed.

The one most of the songs don't mention is the only one who's made the world good and right. Unexpectedly, he simply moved in with us, loved us, and made a way out of the garbage heap—a way that cost him his life.

Opie Doesn't Live Here Anymore

If anyone should be screaming "NOT FAIR!" it should be him.

So perhaps we've been trained to expect too much of the wrong thing from Christmas. When the one whose birth we celebrate called us to "come and follow," he also told us that our following would involve carrying a cross. Life's not easy. Life's not fair. We're not always supposed to be feeling happy, good, and warm inside. Each year—and this year especially—I'm given the gift of learning more about what it is that we celebrate.

This year, the gift of suffering by watching someone I love deal with the gift of suffering has opened my eyes to some pretty amazing stuff.

It's the bad that makes Christmas so good.

My Dad . . .

Blog; June 16, 2006

A strange Father's Day indeed. This year both Lisa and I are thinking about and experiencing Father's Day in new and different ways. Lisa's dad is lying in a Pittsburgh hospital bed fighting cancer that's spread through his body and now into his brain. My dad's living in a nursing care facility

here in Lancaster (Pennsylvania), something that, quite frankly, I never imagined possible.

With experiences like these, you can't help but process the events of your life

without the "take it for granted" sense of entitlement that somehow just happens when blessings have been showered on you so regularly and for so long that you don't even know you've been in the shower. Now I'm experiencing the opposite blessing that comes with watching pain and suffering—the blessing of consciously thinking about and thanking God for every little minute, movement, and breath.

> I remember—almost frame-by-frame, with great detail—that simple little act of letting us in and then him sitting in his recliner. The next time I saw him he was fighting for his life.

One of the last memories I have of my dad with his full health comes from a Monday night last October. Lisa and I popped in on my parents for a short visit before heading west to Pittsburgh for the National Youth Workers Convention. I knocked on their door, watched the porch light come on, and saw the top half of my dad's head appear in the window at the top of their front door. He made one of his usual funny faces, opened the door, said "Hello Walt and Lisa" with some humorous inflection, and ushered us in. I remember—almost frame-by-frame, with great detail—that simple little act of letting us in and then him sitting in his recliner. The next time I saw him he was fighting for his life in intensive care. He hasn't answered a door since. No longer, I hope, do I take for granted these simple little things that were a part of his everyday life.

The past few months have been a great time of reflection. Lots of memories and stories have come back to me as I've thought about my fifty years with Dad. One

Opie Doesn't Live Here Anymore

of those memories has served me well during my own years of fathering.

Back in 1990 this memory was rekindled thanks to some time spent with my friend Ken Canfield from the National Center for Fathering. Ken had gathered about thirty of us who were ministering to families and dads at the time for a few days of refreshment and reflection. We were sitting in a lodge on the banks of Wisconsin's Lake Geneva when Ken asked us each to share our most memorable moments with our own dads. The men in the room were an amazing bunch, and the stories were riveting and emotional—all of them testimony to the life-shaping power of fathers.

When it was my turn to speak, I decided to pull one story from the pool of my favorites. The power of my dad's example and love blessed me with the dilemma of having several stories from which to choose. I thought back to a time when I was only about four or five. I don't exactly remember this happening, although I do remember the setting very well. My memory of this one particular incident comes from my dad's vulnerability and willingness to tell the story as a reminder to himself, and others, of the importance of spending time with your kids.

The setting is one I'll never forget. It was just outside the sanctuary of the church my father was pastoring. In official church lingo, we call the foyer, or gathering place at the back of the sanctuary, the narthex. Each and every Sunday morning after pronouncing the benediction, Dad would walk from the chancel to the doors that separated the sanctuary from the narthex. I remember proudly watching him walk down the aisle, a big and powerful man dressed in his black chancel robe. From my seat next to the aisle, I sensed his power in the breeze I felt after he passed. When the music stopped, I would run to the back of the church to stand with my dad. I would assume a position in front of him and between his long legs. Then I'd pull the folds of that robe around me until only my face was showing, leaving me looking like a timid baby kangaroo sitting in its mother's pouch. I can distinctly remember looking up and watching my dad's huge, muscular, hairy forearm extend out of the robe's sleeve as he shook each parishioner's hand.

> She followed up with one of those "test questions" older parishioners ask the preacher's kid. "Do you love Jesus today?" Without even thinking about it, I shot back "No!"

One particular Sunday, as Dad tells the story, an older woman, who was one of the church's pillars, bent over and looked at me after shaking my father's hand. She reached out and took my hand, shaking it and asking me, "How are you today, Walter?" Dad says I replied "Fine." Then, not satisfied with leaving well enough alone, she followed up with one of those "test questions" older parishioners ask the preacher's kid. "Do you love Jesus today?" Dad says that without even thinking about it, I shot back "No!" Once the dear lady composed herself, picked her teeth up off the floor, and put them back in her mouth (that part's not true!), she was smart enough to follow up on my negative and surprising answer. "Why don't you love Jesus today, Walter?" Dad says I

Opie Doesn't Live Here Anymore

was again quick with my response: "Because he stole my daddy." Hmmm.

When they got home from church, my surprised father asked my mother what she thought the interchange meant. My mom went on to speculate that maybe I was a bit put out by the fact that Dad was out doing God's work almost every night of the week, rather than being home spending time with me. The good news is that the incident became a teachable moment that would shape the rest of my dad's life and ministry. He quickly told his church board that things would be changing drastically. Consequently, I remember my childhood as one filled with great memories of doing things with Dad, something that wouldn't be the case if he hadn't been home. As a benefit, I got the blessing of a great example. God's Spirit was not only using the words of a child to challenge his dad, but God's Spirit would use those words to challenge that boy himself.

> **The good news is that the incident became a teachable moment that would shape the rest of my dad's life and ministry.**

After relating this story to the men in that lodge, I sat back and listened as the others in the circle took their turns talking about their dads. One other man told a church narthex story. He originally had passed on telling a story for the simple reason that his father had taken off when he was a very young boy. He had no stories to tell, he said. Pass. But Ken came back and asked him to relate his most memorable moment with a man. Like mine, his story took the rest of the guys in that group to the back of a church immediately following a service. A fatherless little boy, he would stand against the same spot on the wall while waiting for his mother to emerge out of the crowd to take him home. Only five years old at the time, he felt lost in the sea of big people. He doesn't even remember people noticing him or talking to him as he stood there alone . . . except for the Sunday morning that would yield his most memorable moment with a man.

An older man waiting for his wife saw the young boy leaning against the wall. The boy spotted the man at the same time and watched as he walked over, knelt down to eye level, and then made a connection. The man reached out and put his hand on the boy's head, tousled his hair, and asked, "How are you doing today, sport?" And that was it. No exchange of names. No other conversation. Nothing. Sadly, that was the most significant memory of childhood time spent with a man that this fellow in our group could muster up.

I realized I was blessed—and still am. I hope I am doing the same for my own four kids. Each and every time I visit my dad, I take a conscious look at that right forearm. Still hairy, it's not as big and strong as it was when it would poke out of his robe after the Sunday morning service. His "always-shake-hands-like-a-man-and-not-a-fish" grip is gone. No longer does our handshake extend into a wrestling match to see who can squeeze so hard that the other "gives."

But the strength of his example is stronger than ever.

Picture Box Thoughts

Blog; June 6, 2006

It's been two years since I've been through our picture boxes (we have three of them now in our house). We're one of those families that takes lots of pictures, very few of which ever wind up neatly organized or stuffed with some sense of order into photo albums. That used to bother me a bit, but now I just pretend that my time spent going through the boxes is like a treasure hunt in which I find jewels and gems of memories that seem like they happened just yesterday.

The last time I spent hours going through the boxes was June 2004. That's the year Josh graduated. This year it's Bethany's turn. She graduates tomorrow night and I've been busy putting together the expected "slide show that Dad does for each of us kids when we graduate from high school." I load several dozen pictures, some video clips, and a carefully chosen soundtrack into a PowerPoint presentation. At some point during Bethany's graduation party this Saturday, I'll pull everyone together for a few minutes of "oohing" and "aahing" as we view her eighteen years condensed into fifteen minutes.

My time looking through the pictures and videos is always a bit emotional for me. On a couple of occasions during the last two weeks I've come up from the basement after hunting through the treasure chest only to be met in the kitchen by my kids. By now they all know what I'm doing down there, and they tend to harass me a bit for my glassy eyes and quiet demeanor that come from the tears I've shed while alone downstairs with the memories. I guess it's to be expected. After all, they really don't understand how fast life travels.

I remember one time hearing Ken Davis say that on the day his daughter was born, he picked her up, cradled her in his arms, and stared into her face. Then he blinked. When he opened his eyes, she was a young lady. When I heard him say that, I didn't fully get it. My kids were still little. Now I understand. Some day my kids will get it as well. But for now, they tease me a bit. That sometimes pounds the message home more, especially after spending hours of looking at them when they are young, then coming upstairs to see them fully grown, teasing me with their adult voices that come from their adult bodies. Where have the years gone?

> **On the day his daughter was born, he picked her up, cradled her in his arms, and stared into her face. Then he blinked. When he opened his eyes, she was a young lady.**

In a couple of months, Bethany will follow the footsteps of her two older siblings and head off to college. Hard to believe, but it's happening. As we spend the next few days celebrating this milestone in her life, I will tell her I'm proud of her. We'll pray for her, thanking God for her past, and asking him to bless her future. And, we'll thank God that he's called Bethany to be his own. Finally, we'll continue to pray that, for the rest of her life, she wouldn't—as John Piper says—waste her life on "fatal success."

There's a picture posted with this blog that I found in the box this week. If I found a favorite, this is it. For me, it's gold. It was taken sixteen years ago on a summer vacation at a lake in Maine. I never knew it was being taken because my back was to the camera. Bethany and

Opie Doesn't Live Here Anymore

I were spending some alone time, moments out on the dock as the evening sun was starting to go down. Lisa must have snuck up behind us to snap the photo.

I blinked, and now she's graduating. God bless you, Bethany.

EMBRACING THE COLLISION

How long, O Lord? Will you forget me forever? How long will you hide your face from me? How long must I wrestle with my thoughts and every day have sorrow in my heart? How long will my enemy triumph over me? Look on me and answer, O Lord my God. Give light to my eyes, or I will sleep in death; my enemy will say, "I have overcome him," and my foes will rejoice when I fall. But I trust in your unfailing love; my heart rejoices in your salvation. I will sing to the Lord, for he has been good to me. (Psalm 13)

But God demonstrates his own love for us in this: While we were still sinners, Christ died for us. (Romans 5:8)

Consider it pure joy, my brothers, whenever you face trials of many kinds, because you know that the testing of your faith develops perseverance. Perseverance must finish its work so that you may be mature and complete, not lacking anything. (James 1:2-4)

1. WHY DO YOU THINK MANY IN OUR CULTURE BELIEVE THAT LOVE IS MERELY A FEELING? What's wrong with this understanding?

Opie Doesn't Live Here Anymore

2. AS I WROTE IN THE LETTER TO MY DAUGHTER, it's not easy to live a life marked by grace. What does such a life look like? How do you struggle with living this way?

3. CONSIDER PRAYING *Let my heart be broken by the things that break the heart of God.* Why is this a dangerous prayer?

4. DO YOU THINK WE'VE COME TO EXPECT TOO MUCH of the wrong things from Christmas? What have you been trained to expect?

5. "WHEN THE ONE WHOSE BIRTH WE CELEBRATE CALLED US TO 'come and follow,' he also told us that our following would involve carrying a cross." Is this the message we explain to our kids? How have you done this? How can you do it more?

DESPERATE TIMES, DIVINE MEASURES

WHEN OUR LOCAL LANCASTER COUNTY community was rocked by the execution-style shootings of Amish schoolgirls in October 2006, the world was fixated on the story and consumed with the question "Why?" One local newspaper ran a simply stated, oversized headline that read, "Innocence Lost." Because as Westerners we've lived our lives in relative peace and comfort, we're stunned when evil rears its head in such a horrifying way.

I've come to realize that our surprise, and the resulting questions, are most likely rooted in the fact that we've bought into and believed a foundational lie about the nature of our world. Rather than viewing its inhabitants as polluted by sin and groaning for healing (Romans 8:22), we've somehow come to believe that people are inherently good. Consequently, we're surprised when people and things go terribly wrong. We're left scratching our heads in shock and disbelief as we ask each other "Why?" But we really aren't innocent. If we were, we wouldn't need a Redeemer. When we understand the true nature of the world through the eyes of God's Word, perhaps the question we should be asking is "Why doesn't this happen more?"

Because of the reality of evil in the world, we live in desperate times. But they actually are no more or less desperate than they've been since the moment human rebellion undid God's perfect world. Perhaps we see them as more desperate because we've allowed our peace and comfort to blind us from seeing the world as it really is. We've been lulled into buying a lie. When we see the world as it really is, we'll be awestruck by God's amazing grace, evidenced not only in the rescue mission of Jesus Christ that we experience on a personal level, but also in his willingness to restrain evil and keep relationships from running the ugly course they would take if he had not loved his creation enough to intervene. These are the divine measures God has taken to undo the reality of our desperate times.

As those rescued into the fold of God's people, we're called to follow Christ and serve as salt and light in the midst of the world's desperate darkness and decay. In effect, we've been called and sent as part of that divine measure to penetrate society and influence the world for good. In the end, the divine measures will unfold completely. All of God's creation will be restored to its original glory and the evil that shouldn't surprise us now will be banished from creation forever (Revelation 21:1-5).

But in the "now" and "in-between" in which we find ourselves living, we must follow and represent the Savior, answering evil by living God's good.

Again...

Blog; October 3, 2006

Editor's note: On the morning of October 2, 2006, a truck driver armed with three firearms barricaded himself in a one-room Amish schoolhouse in Nickel Mines, Pennsylvania, and took a number of students hostage. After releasing all boys, a pregnant woman, and three other women with infants in arms, Charles Roberts shot and killed five girls, and critically wounded five others, before killing himself.

No doubt you've heard the news about what happened here in Lancaster County yesterday. The massacre at the Amish schoolhouse was the third multiple-murder incident—involving children and teens as either victims or perpetrators—to rock our community in less than a year. After each I've had the same thought: *I'm very sad, but not surprised.* The spirit in which I say that is not one that's arrogant. Instead, it is one that recognizes that this is our world, this is the culture we've created, and this is the fruit of the sinful and fallen human heart. Looking at our world through the eyes of biblical faith and biblical history, this kind of thing is to be expected. If these types of events should spark surprise, it's the surprise that they aren't happening more. Regardless, what's happened is absolutely horrific.

As the world focuses attention on our local Amish community—a community that doesn't watch or listen to the news—I'm hoping that what doesn't get lost in all the sensationalistic media coverage is the amazing grace and forgiveness these peaceful people are sure to give, and to give quickly. In a day and age when high-profile and outspoken Christians continue to exercise indiscretions that encourage the world to scoff, the Amish are a breath of fresh air and a shining example of humility.

This morning, one of our CPYU friends, Jonas Beiler, appeared on *The Today Show*. Jonas spent yesterday counseling the families of the children who were so brutally attacked. When asked about the families, Jonas replied by describing not so much the grief they must feel, but the forgiveness that's already flowing from their community. Never have I seen people who model Christ-like forgiveness as the Amish do. Jonas got me thinking about a story we shared with you a few years ago. Written by my friend, youth pastor Joel Kime, the story describes in gripping detail the forgiveness Joel experienced after a horrific accident that left a young Amish woman dead.

> **When asked about the families, Jonas replied by describing not so much the grief they must feel, but the forgiveness that's already flowing from their community. Never have I seen people who model Christ-like forgiveness as the Amish do.**

Hopefully, the events of the last twenty-four hours will serve to remind us that we live in a culture of violence. Sadly, we celebrate violence so much and so often through the media that we are training and socializing our kids into leading violent lives. While I'm all for free speech, it only works when those doing the talking exercise responsibility. I also hope that the events of the last twenty-four hours show us the power of living in a culture of forgiveness. Yesterday, today, and tomorrow, we're sure to catch glimpses of the kingdom of God breaking through in all its power and glory as those who have been terribly wronged reach out in the midst of tremendous grief—to forgive.

What a Contrast!

Blog; October 5, 2006

Yesterday morning, I opened my paper to catch up on developments related to what has become known worldwide as "the Amish Schoolhouse Shootings." The paper covered the many prayer services that took place on Tuesday night in various spots around the county. It was a joy to read about how our local Christian community is surrounding the families of the victims and the shooter with prayer, love, and assistance. In addition, I read one of the moving stories that has been recounted numerous times around here and in the worldwide media. While it bothers me that the media and other opportunists looking for the limelight have descended on our community, the coverage has afforded opportunities for the message of God's kingdom to be spread far and wide. This includes the wonderful story of what happened on Tuesday at the home of shooter, Charles Roberts. An Amish man came to the family's home and embraced Roberts's father. "We will forgive you," the Amish man said.

The Amish commitment to handle death in a God-honoring way is amazing. One Amish woman decided to appear on camera for the sole reason of telling the world that their focus through all of this is on Christ. Their determination and capacity to forgive is truly Christ-like. I have been constantly reminded of Christ's words to the repentant criminal on the cross during their dying hours, the command to turn the other cheek, the admonition to forgive seventy times seven, and the astounding depth of divine forgiveness I've experienced in my own life.

An Opportunity I Wish I Never Had

Blog; October 6, 2005

Today I am emotionally drained. Last night I chatted and prayed with a group of parents I had not met before. They are the parents of three teenagers—Jennifer Blouch, Daniel Abernethy, and Jon Gettle—who made the painful decision to end their lives in the past few months.

I was in Lebanon, Pennsylvania, at the invitation of the good folks at the Mental Health Association of Lebanon County, and of Scott and Donna Blouch, Jennifer's father and mother. I had been asked by Scott to speak about the problem of teen suicide. His hope is that he can somehow take the pain of his situation and turn it into something good for the kids in his community. I prayed and worked hard in an effort to figure out what I should say and how I should say it.

> None of them knew anything was wrong. None of them suspected their child was thinking about suicide. Each one was taken completely by surprise.

More than five hundred people—mostly teens—showed up. I spoke to them about the brokenness so many young people feel in their lives and God's initiative in history to bring life and hope. On my ride back home I thought a lot about the kids who were there. . . .

Desperate Times, Divine Measures

Lord, give them hope and make them whole. But more than that, I thought about those parents.

None of them knew anything was wrong. None of them suspected their child was thinking about suicide. Each one was taken completely by surprise. And, their lives changed forever in an instant. But what struck me most about these parents was their resolve to turn their mourning into dancing for someone else by embarking on a crusade to stem the tide of teen suicide.

Scott and Donna poured their hearts into last night's event. In addition, Scott and his pastor have been visiting area schools to speak openly with kids about suicide. Daniel Abernethy's mom, Beverly, is serving as the director/coordinator of "The Yellow Ribbon" teen suicide prevention program. The program helps kids crying out for understanding to get the assistance and intervention they so desperately need. And Cathy Gettle, whose son Jon was a victim of middle school bullying, is now a speaker on "Teasing, Bullying, and Teen Suicide."

Although I'm emotionally drained, I came away from last night with a clear sense and new resolve to spread this word when it comes to teens: pray and watch. Suicide is a real and growing problem. I saw its wake last night. And pray for those caught in that wake. Thank you, Scott and Donna, for what you did for your community and its kids last night. While we all wish there had been no reason for us to get together like we did, the sad reality is that it's necessary.

Today my prayer is this: *God, may you richly bless the Blouchs, the Gettles, and the Abernethys with a deep sense of your mercy, peace, and healing grace.*

Opie Doesn't Live Here Anymore

DANCING TO DESPAIR

Blog; July 12, 2004

I was there at Hersheypark Stadium in the midst of thirty thousand people last Saturday night—Section 26, Row E, Seat 34—right next to the aisle. We got there early so we wouldn't miss anything. I like to spend lots of time watching the crowd. Binoculars come in real handy for that.

We opted not to park in the stadium lot. We missed all the pre-concert partying that way. I parked in a lot at the outlet mall. There was a little bit of partying going on over there too. As we cut through a restaurant parking lot, a couple of fifteen-year-olds playing Hacky Sack asked me if I "needed some." I told them no and kept walking so we could get into the stadium.

> **As we cut through a restaurant parking lot, a couple of fifteen-year-olds playing Hacky Sack asked me if I "needed some." I told them no and kept walking so we could get into the stadium.**

The opening band, Galactic, played a short set to a fairly disengaged crowd that was still filing in and fairly sparse. They could jam—they sounded a lot like The Allman Brothers. At eight o'clock, Dave Matthews and his band took the stage and the crowd went crazy. I'm crazy in a reserved kind of way, so much so that one drunk guy stumbling up the aisle next to me stopped, looked me in the eye, and yelled, "Stop looking so happy!" OK, so I don't jump around and dance. I like to sit, stand, and quietly listen. Plus, if you ever saw me jump around and dance you'd realize that, by sitting still, I'm saving everyone near me a good dose of pain and agony.

I love DMB's music because of its creativity. Those guys can play. Their creativity reminds me of our awesome creator and the amazing variety of ways he's imaged himself into us and made us just a little lower than the heavenly beings.

But still, it was hard to listen to DMB this time around. I was distracted by the multisensory activity all around me. I spent most of my time looking through the binoculars at the faces of those who seemed to be spinning their wheels in a search for redemption by looking no further than to Dave for a savior. Living from concert to concert for these folks, the feeling's good for a three-hour set, and then it's back to the grind of a meaningless existence.

Then there was the sound of some people singing along to every one of Dave's words. I couldn't help but wonder for each person: what does it mean to them? And there was the unmistakable smell of a DMB concert. Unlike the smell at a baseball game—that "I'm-not-sure-why-it's-so-pleasing" combination of cigar smoke, watered-down beer, hot dogs, and glove leather—this odor had only two ingredients: the aforementioned watered-down beer (lots of it) and the smoke (lots of that too) coming from the folks who had stopped by my fifteen-year-old friends in the parking lot because they "needed some."

The crowd was particularly unruly. Especially saddening was the emptiness I saw in the group of ten or so high school students who filled the aisle for about forty-five minutes in a drunken and pot-induced stupor. I couldn't help but think that I was looking at someone's sons or daughters. It hurt even more to realize that they were

Opie Doesn't Live Here Anymore

more than likely cut off from their heavenly Father. The empty faces were harrowing.

> Saddening was the emptiness I saw in the group of ten or so high school students who filled the aisle for about forty-five minutes in a drunken and pot-induced stupor. I couldn't help but think that I was looking at someone's sons or daughters.

The concert ended and I hurried our group out, taking the shortcut back to our parking lot to beat the traffic. We timed it perfectly, passing the backstage gate as Dave's bus pulled out just fifteen feet from us. There he was, standing in the fully lit front window, smiling and waving in the direction of the thirty to forty of us who happened to be standing there. Drummer Carter Beauford's bus came by next and he was smiling at us too. That guy never stops smiling.

On the way home we got to talking about the whole experience and what we saw. Dave Matthews looks like such a happy guy. He loves what he does. He loves his fans. His music is so upbeat. But lyrically—it's nothing but darkness. I was thinking about how I was looking through my binoculars and down my aisle for three hours at a stadium full of people as I wondered again and again: *What does it all mean to them, and why do they like it?*

My conclusion was what it's been for a while—they're dancing and listening as a diversion from their despair. Even though they may appear to be so far from the truth, I know that they have "eternity in [their] hearts"

(Ecclesiastes 3:11). They are deeply longing for God, and most don't even know it. I look at them and, with Solomon, realize that without God, "who can eat or find enjoyment?" (Ecclesiastes 2:25).

It was another bittersweet night. Good music, insightful yet oftentimes despairing lyrics, and another powerful reminder that without God there's really no way to make sense of life and find lasting meaning . . . but people sure do try. For me, it's another reminder of why I do what I do, how to pray, and how grateful I am for the opportunity I have to do both.

Deep and Wide

Blog; March 20, 2006

C.S. Lewis said that "No man knows how bad he is till he has tried very hard to be good." Man's depravity— that's something I've been thinking about quite a bit for the last few days. One of those phone calls you never expect to receive was what got me thinking.

A friend . . . a good friend for almost thirty years . . . a man who I have watched love and serve the Lord, as well as loving and serving others . . . a man who for a few years was a trusted partner in ministry to college students . . . was arrested and charged, along with four others, for involuntary deviate sexual intercourse with a male minor. Right now he's sitting in a jail cell awaiting tomorrow's arraignment. Since getting the call my heart has been heavy and my head has been full of questions.

My thoughts on depravity were fueled again as I sat on the sidelines to watch my oldest son play lacrosse

Opie Doesn't Live Here Anymore

last Saturday. His Messiah College team was playing at Lynchburg College. Kudos go out to the winning Lynchburg squad, which played a great and disciplined game on the field. But it was what I saw and heard across the field that added to my already aching heart.

> Without standards or absolutes, civility is a thing of the past, and our depravity is unleashed, deep and wide, in a celebratory fashion for all the world to see.

There, in front of the student dorms, was a large contingent of students whose actions went far beyond healthy school spirit. I watched as they went in and out of their dorms to fill their glasses during the game. Many appeared to be intoxicated. Profanity seemed to be the order of the day. Our team and our fans were the targets of unrestrained insults. At one point I heard chants of "Where's your Messiah now?" and "There is no Messiah!" coming from the other side. It got so bad that some of the opposing players' parents and even one of the school's coaches apologized to our contingent for what we saw and heard. And what we saw and heard was indicative of where our culture is going. Without standards or absolutes, civility is a thing of the past, and our depravity is unleashed, deep and wide, in a celebratory fashion for all the world to see.

And so last week I was reminded twice of the fact that sin affects the very core of every man, woman, and child. Well, it wasn't only those two times, if I'm going to be honest with you. The reminders fly at me every time I pause to look deep within every nook and cranny of my own heart. Yes, depravity runs deep and wide in me. In fact, some of my thoughts about those who faced me on the other side of that lacrosse field revealed that the place where I really sat was right there in their midst. Can I really think I'm any better just because I wasn't shouting back?

And if I'm honest with myself when I look into the face of my fallen friend, I can't go down the pharisaical road I so often and easily travel. Instead, I can only look into my mirror and humbly say, "There, but for the grace of God, go I." So I continue to pray, not only for my friend—but for myself.

What's Going On? Reflections from 9/11

Youthculture@today, December 2001

More than thirty of pop music's biggest stars converged on a New York City recording studio during the first week of September. Already in town for the MTV *Video Music Awards*, this diverse group—representing the entire pop music spectrum, including Britney Spears, Bono, Ja Rule, Jennifer Lopez, Fred Durst, Michael Stipe, and many others—was lending its voice to a musical project that was to benefit AIDS research and awareness. Over the course of several days, the group recorded a remake of Marvin Gaye's 1971 classic "What's Going On"—a song full of questions about that era's confusing mix of social problems.

Before the recording was finished, however, the ground beneath the artists' feet literally rumbled with shock waves from the horrifying events of September 11.

The emotional shock waves led the benefit's producers to change their plans. Within a matter of days, the finished

Opie Doesn't Live Here Anymore

project hit the MTV video heavy-rotation playlist with a shifted focus and a sense of relevance that just days before was unimaginable. Coupled with an ongoing stream of gut-wrenching video images taken at Ground Zero on September 11, the lyrics of "What's Going On" verbalized the collective questioning of a shocked world that was asking, again and again: *Brother, brother, brother / There's far too many of you dying / You know we've got to find a way / To bring some lovin' here today . . .* [1]

No doubt, history will remember September 11, 2001, as a day when so much more than the direction of a music video shifted. Millions of people around the world—including children and teens—sat and watched, shook their heads in confusion and disbelief, and asked: *What's going on?*

> **How can we explain the unexplainable to our kids when we don't understand it ourselves? What would God like us to take away from this?**

As a father faced with the responsibility of explaining the day's events to my own kids, I found myself asking several additional questions: How can we hope to make any sense of such a horrendous act? Where can we go to find answers? How can we explain the unexplainable to our kids when we don't understand it ourselves? What would God like us to take away from this?

Since September 11, you've probably seen and heard countless commentators and experts offer their thoughts, answers, and opinions. They've told us how much our world has changed. Among other things, we've been told that our sense of invulnerability has been shaken to the core, we can no longer feel safe, and yes, there are some very evil people in our world. Without a doubt, the shock waves of 9/11 were felt around the globe and, in many ways, things have changed.

Late that night—glued to the television as it replayed the horrifying images of the day's events—I jotted a stream of seemingly disjointed sentences in my journal. Each sentence captured a glimpse of what I was seeing and feeling as I stared in disbelief at the images. I don't come close to knowing the answers, but I believe my random late-night scribblings helped me understand bits and pieces of what was going on.

> **"I can't believe I'm not weeping over this. I'm numb. It's almost like I'm sitting here watching an Arnold Schwarzenegger or Bruce Willis movie."**

As I've pondered and processed the words I wrote on 9/11 (in italics below, followed by some clarifying thoughts since), I've realized that the day's ugly events probably didn't change the world as much as we might think. Instead, the terrorist attacks have changed us by opening our eyes to some present realities our culture had forgotten long before the attacks.

I've seen this all somewhere before. Sadly, I think I've been desensitized. Even though the death toll was huge, I was almost numb to it. While watching the Twin Towers collapse on live television with my coworker, Cliff, I turned and said, "I can't believe I'm not weeping over this. I'm numb. It's almost like I'm sitting here watching an Arnold Schwarzenegger or Bruce Willis movie." Later that night,

I shed tears alone. But in the weeks since September 11, most people I've talked to have told me they felt the same surprising numbness.

I think we've been desensitized. Perhaps it's Hollywood's fascination with portraying bigger, better, and more realistic disasters on the big and small screens. Perhaps it's our fascination with watching so much of this stuff. Sadly, I've heard too many stories of kids who—as they watched the towers collapse—responded with "Cool!" Unfortunately, they weren't sitting in a darkened theater, munching popcorn. This was real, and they didn't even know it. This desensitization has led many, including myself, to desire to visit Ground Zero to see it for themselves—not to fulfill some morbid fascination, but just to know that it really did happen and to experience the depth of pain we all should feel. Should we be surprised?

I need to rethink the object of my faith. As I watch the endless replays of the day's events, I'm struck deeply by what each of the objects that crashed to earth represents in American life. Airplanes: not only a symbol of our growing technological expertise, but our high level of mobility. The World Trade Center's Twin Towers: recognized around the world as monuments to capitalism and the financial security and happiness that comes from seeking salvation through the American Dream. The Pentagon: the nerve center of the most advanced and powerful military and defense establishment in the world.

How easy it is to be lulled into a false sense of security and invulnerability by the knowledge we possess, the things we've accumulated, the powerful muscles we can flex. What's going on? Perhaps we've made the same mistake we've been making ever since our self-imposed eviction from the Garden of Eden—we've placed our faith in false gods. How easily they can crumble in minutes, before our eyes. In the midst of all this change, the unchanging God, the only one worthy of our worship, is still God. Should we be surprised?

Deep down, people are not good. "What kind of people would do this sort of thing?" That question's been asked over and over since September 11. If we buy the lie that people are fundamentally good, the day's events leave us scratching our heads in disbelief. We believe evil somehow isolated and manifested itself inside the hearts and minds of only a few "bad" people—in this case the twenty or so terrorists who came here from halfway around the world to carry out a diabolical plan. Yes, by the grace of God we are all capable of doing what's good, right, honorable, and true. But the thoughts in my mind, the darkness in my heart, the locks on my doors, the police on my street, the courts in my county, the history of wars and conflicts, the images of smoking rubble on my television—all point to the fact that what the Bible teaches us is so true, that the seeds of sin are present in every human heart. Mine and yours included.

> **What's going on? Perhaps we've made the same mistake we've been making ever since our self-imposed eviction from the Garden of Eden—we've placed our faith in false gods.**

If we understand that no part of any person walking the earth is left untainted by our individual and collective rebellion against God, then we understand that the heart of a hijacker is really no darker than the one that beats in

Opie Doesn't Live Here Anymore

us. "What kind of evil people would do this sort of thing?" People whose nature is really no different from mine. I look deep inside myself. Then I look at what happened on September 11. Should we be surprised?

> **If we understand that no part of any person walking the earth is left untainted by our individual and collective rebellion against God, then we understand that the heart of a hijacker is really no darker than the one that beats in us.**

We need God. On September 6, I was interviewed live on a Midwest radio station. I was discussing an exciting trend in today's youth culture: the growing awareness of and interest in spirituality among today's teenagers. We also talked about a not-so-exciting trend in today's church culture: the growing gap between the faith we profess with our lips and the faith we live in our everyday lives. The host, while talking about our need for a deepened dependence on God, asked what I thought it would take for our nation's Christian teenagers and adults to get to the point where we would fully rely on God with a faith that is integrated into all of life. Judging from how many times I've been asked the question, it's a real issue. I answered as I always do: "What we need to deepen and cement our faith, I'm afraid, is a national crisis that brings us to our knees in awareness of our deep need for God."

Our need for God came to mind several times on September 11. At 8:45 AM I walked into our office after driving a vanload of CPYU banquet invitations to the post office. Do you know what those invitations advertised as the banquet's theme? "I Need God: Youth

Culture's Cry for Healing." Ten minutes after returning to the office, I turned on the TV and sat there throughout the day, watching our nation's self-awareness of this need for God grow by the minute. Mine certainly did. When Billy Graham spoke at the National Memorial Service in Washington, he sent a powerful message to millions watching live on TV: "We've come together in this service to confess our need of God. We've always needed God from the very beginning of this nation. But today, we need him especially." Should we be surprised?

If past experience is any indicator, today, sadly, is just one big interruption, and life will go on as usual. I hope not. I can't let that happen to me. I live in the most bountiful nation on the face of the earth. Our wealth, freedom, and opportunity are unsurpassed. Consequently, it's easy to become so self-absorbed that if we didn't personally know someone injured or killed in the attacks, we might go right back to life as usual, forgetting the many important lessons this crisis can teach. I'm afraid that might be happening.

My recent conversations with secondary school teachers and administrators indicate that while initially there was a sense of heightened fear among students, it's been diminishing quickly. Yes, we need to get back to life as usual. But life as usual needs to be shaped by mindful intention to learn from this event. God has lessons for us to learn regarding our need for repentance and our dependence on him. Hopefully, we won't be people who call on God only when our everyday going gets rough. There are no atheists in foxholes, but when the firing stops, the dust settles, and the rubble's cleared, it's usually back to business as usual. Should we be surprised?

Opie Doesn't Live Here Anymore

As the sun was going down on September 11, dozens of amateur vocalists converged on the steps of the United States Capitol in Washington, DC. The diverse group of members of Congress stood together in an act of bipartisan unity and joined their voices in an emotional version of "God Bless America." Their musical prayer brought tears to my eyes.

> When the firing stops, the dust settles, and the rubble's cleared, it's usually back to business as usual. Should we be surprised?

In the days and weeks since, millions of Americans have sung along. The lyrics verbalize the collective prayer of a nation in shock. Yes, I thought, we do need God's blessing.

But I also believe we'll be tempted to sing the tune with a preconceived idea of how God can and should bless America. If those notions of blessing include a growing economy, military victory, and international supremacy, I think we're praying for the wrong things. All we've done is ask God to meet what we believe to be our needs on our terms. Granted, God may choose to bring what we see as blessing in those areas. But our prayer should be for God to shower his blessing, in his time, in his way. That's always what's best for us and always what we need. If what we need is increased dependence on God, he might just have to clear our view by getting some of the obstacles out of the way. Then, perhaps, we'll raise our voices in unison to sing the words of the psalmist: "God is our refuge and strength, an ever-present help in trouble" (Psalm 46:1).

That, I believe, is what we should hope and pray is going on. And if we reach that point, we should be extremely grateful.

THE MILLENNIAL MORAL MESS

Youthculture@today; March 1999

I didn't know her. I didn't know her parents. I had never seen any of them before. But for the few minutes our paths crossed in the small foyer of a local indoor-soccer facility, I witnessed a lesson passed from one generation to the next through the power of parental example.

> **Their impressionable young daughter soaked it all in. Sadly, in their minds, they had done nothing wrong.**

Dad and Mom were openly discussing the need to register their daughter (she appeared to be about ten) for the next soccer season. With money tight and the registration deadline at hand, Dad verbalized his elaborate scheme to deliberately submit the registration form without the necessary payment. A couple of "little" lies and a story about "forgetting" to write a check would give them the extra week to adjust the family budget and get the money together. Mom responded with a big smile and nod of approval. Their impressionable young daughter soaked it all in. Sadly, in their minds, they had done nothing wrong. Even worse, it appeared they thought they were doing the right thing.

Since then, I've pondered how those parents, and others like them, might defend their course of action. Their justification would most likely include a statement

Opie Doesn't Live Here Anymore

I've heard on more than one occasion: "What's the big deal? It's not hurting anybody." I've got to disagree. Maybe that little girl didn't walk out of there with a visible cut or throbbing bruise, but the lie did leave a permanent mark on her heart and mind. And if her mom and dad are consistent at passing on these morally relativistic lessons, the sum total of that education will leave a scar that sets the course for a lifetime of decisions motivated by feelings and expediency, rather than right and wrong.

That youngster is part of the second baby boom (born between 1977 and 1994), a "millennial" generation so large they are only exceeded in number by boomers themselves. While it's still too early to draw final conclusions on who and what millennials will grow up to be and believe, their growing commitment to personally defined standards of morality offers a discouraging peek into a future in which commonly held standards of right and wrong are replaced by personal preference and choice. Already, we see the results, as more than 75 percent of the population believe that absolute truth cannot be known. More than 61 percent believe that sex before marriage is "OK" if both people are "emotionally ready." And 57 percent believe that lying is "sometimes necessary."[2]

A few years ago I had an opportunity to spend a weekend with a couple hundred millennial kids. They had come to a gathering of church youth groups at which I was the featured speaker. The organizers planned a special segment before each of my talks. They had secured spiritually mature student volunteers to give a short reflection and challenge related to my topic. As the weekend unfolded, I was impressed with the insights and wisdom shared by these students—until Saturday night arrived.

I was scheduled to speak about the biblical standards of right and wrong as they relate to God's wonderful gift of sexuality. The time came for the student reflection. Up to the microphone stepped an attractive high school sophomore. She began her remarks by relating the struggle she and her boyfriend of recent months had encountered as they dealt firsthand with the desire to engage in sexual intercourse. Her faith in God was put to the test. Eventually, she told us, they went ahead and had sex. Feeling guilty, they decided to study what God had to say about their behavior. They soon swept their guilt under the rug as they found justification for their continued sexual encounters. "We've talked about it, prayed about it, and looked at the Bible," she said. Then she ended her remarks: "We've concluded that God wants nothing more than for us to feel good and be happy. As a result, we're still having sex."

> As the weekend unfolded, I was impressed with the insights and wisdom shared by these students—until Saturday night arrived.

I sat in my seat stunned. I'd heard all this from kids before—but never in this context. Perhaps more surprising—and revealing—was the response of her peers. They applauded in a manner that was more approving than polite. I watched in silence as the young student walked to her seat with a smile on her face. Needless to say, as I walked to the front of the room, I knew I had my work cut out for me.

Opie Doesn't Live Here Anymore

That young girl was speaking for a generation—churched and unchurched—whose behavior, sexual and otherwise, should be viewed as an expected and faithful expression of a worldview shaped by years of living around consistent moral inconsistency that is hurting them. Today's popular music reflects the moral heartbeat of the millennials. Currently on the record charts, the band Creed, in their song "In America," asks: *What is right or wrong / I don't know who to believe in.*[3] And Sheryl Crow shares this observation in her hit song "Everyday Is a Winding Road": *. . . These are the days when anything goes.*[4]

Yes, we've all got our work cut out for us. Where, though, do we begin? Can we really make a difference? Is there a way to undo this moral mess as we enter the new millennium?

I recently read about a busy dad who came home from a weeklong business trip. He went to his favorite chair to catch up on a stack of accumulated newspapers. Happy that dad was home, his little boy begged his tired father to go outside and play catch. The weary father explained to his disappointed son that he had to read the newspapers. It wasn't long before the little guy came back again to beg his father for some attention. The frustrated dad grabbed a page of the newspaper that was covered with a world map and ripped it into several dozen pieces. Then he handed the pieces to his son in an effort to get him out of his hair. "Here," the dad said. "Go out to the kitchen table and see if you can put this map together." After just a couple of minutes the boy came back and reported that the map was in one piece. In disbelief, the father went out and looked on the table. Sure enough, there sat the completed map of the world. "How'd you do this?" the surprised father asked. "It was easy," the little guy said. "There was a boy's picture on the other side of the map, and I just put it together."

It's overwhelming to look around at a big world marked by increased and serious moral confusion. Where do we begin to undo the world's wrong with a clear sense of God's right? The answer was lying on that kitchen table. Concentrate on investing energy and example in putting children together right—one at a time, and one piece at a time—and the world will take care of itself.

The best place to start is right at home—and by doing the right thing in the foyer at soccer sign-ups.

EMBRACING THE COLLISION

We know that the whole creation has been groaning as in the pains of childbirth right up to the present time.
(Romans 8:22)

My prayer is not that you take them out of the world but that you protect them from the evil one. They are not of the world, even as I am not of it. Sanctify them by the truth; your word is truth. As you sent me into the world, I have sent them into the world. For them I sanctify myself, that they too may be truly sanctified. (John 17:15-19)

Then I saw a new heaven and a new earth, for the first heaven and the first earth had passed away, and there was no longer any sea. . . . And I heard a loud voice from the throne saying, "Now, the dwelling of God is with men, and he will live with them. They will be his people, and God himself will be with them and be their God. . . ." He who was seated on the throne said, "I am making everything new!" Then he said, "Write this down, for these words are trustworthy and true."
(Revelation 21:1, 3, 5)

1. DO YOU AGREE THAT BECAUSE OF OUR OWN PEACE AND COMFORT we've been blinded from seeing the world as it actually is? Why or why not?

2. DO YOU AGREE WITH THE CONCLUSION that musical performers like the Dave Matthews Band are popular because they serve as "diversions from despair"? Are there diversions from despair you've sought in your life? Besides popular music, what are other examples of such diversions in our culture?

3. OFTEN, WE'RE VERY GOOD AT POINTING OUT THE SIN AND DEPRAVITY in others' lives and within our culture, but aren't as quick to do so in our own lives. Why? What steps can you take to remind yourself that the effects of sin run deep within every crevice of our own hearts?

4. HOW CAN THAT KNOWLEDGE HELP YOU AND I become the people God wants us to be?

Opie Doesn't Live Here Anymore

THE WORLD PULLED OVER OUR EYES

THERE'S A FUNNY SEGMENT IN ONE OF OUR family videos that serves as an all-too-powerful reminder of how I've sometimes chosen to live my life. It was Nate's seventh birthday and a dozen of his buddies took turns using an old broomstick to whack away at a piñata I had hung from our backyard swing set. Blindfolded, not one of the disoriented little fellas ever hit the candy-filled, papier-mâché donkey. In fact, they didn't even come close . . . until we ended the exercise in futility by letting them all pound away without the cloth over their eyes.

When we choose to view life through the blindfold of lies—a ridiculously silly-sounding reality, yet one that we all too often embrace—we miss out on seeing what's really happening. There's a scene in *The Matrix* where Morpheus (Laurence Fishburne) explains to the young Neo, his soon-to-be protégé, what the Matrix really is. It's a complex system of lies that is, Morpheus says, "everywhere. . . . It's all around us, here even in this room. You can see it out your window, or on your television. You feel it when you go to work, or go to church, or pay your taxes." Then Morpheus explains the result of wearing the blindfold of the Matrix: "It is the world that has been pulled over your eyes to blind you from the truth." [1]

> **Miraculously, my eyes have been opened and healed. Yet I far too frequently choose to wear a blindfold that is both attractive and convincing.**

And when we choose to wear it, we find ourselves walking through life sightlessly—even though we're convinced there's absolutely nothing wrong with our vision. Consequently, we misplace our priorities—and embrace idolatry—without even knowing it.

Opie Doesn't Live Here Anymore

We need to have the blindfolds removed. Our eyes must be healed. When we respond in the affirmative to Jesus' invitation to "Come and follow me," not only are our eyes healed and opened for the first time, but we embark on a lifetime of keeping our eyes focused on the incarnate and written Word. All of life is to be viewed through the crystal clear corrective lens of a biblical worldview. Rather than looking at and living in our world's Matrix, we are called to look at, embrace, and live in the truth.

Miraculously, my eyes have been opened and healed. Yet I far too frequently choose to wear a blindfold that is both attractive and convincing. Then I'm left flailing away and doing life in a manner that doesn't come anywhere close to what it should be. What follows are thoughts prompted by some of those "world-pulled-over-our-eyes" experiences that are not only personal but also woven through the fabric of our contemporary culture.

OUR CHEATIN' HEART

Youthculture@today; March 2000

They appeared together on the cover of *Sports Illustrated* after being named "1999 Sportswomen of the Year." And yes, on July 10, I was one of forty-four million American television viewers on the edge of my seat watching the U.S. Women's soccer team try to win the World Cup final against China.

After the game ended in a scoreless tie, it all came down to a shootout. Some say the key play that won it for the U.S. was the amazing diving save by goalkeeper Briana Scurry on Liu Ying's shot. Like millions of others, I got caught up in the moment and jumped out of my seat with a "thrill of victory" yell. It was exciting!

But for me, the thrill of the U.S. team's amazing victory quickly subsided when Scurry openly admitted her decision to increase her chances to make the save by ignoring the rules regarding penalty kicks. Just as her opponent approached the ball, Scurry took two quick steps forward to cut down Ying's angle on the goal. The tactic worked as Scurry was then able to dive to her left to tip the shot wide of the goal. Even though the referee didn't catch the foul, Scurry had violated the rule that allows goalkeepers to move only laterally, not forward, before a kick.

In the days and weeks that followed, sports fans, columnists, and talk show hosts debated whether Scurry had in fact "cheated." I was distressed by her comments on the incident. "If I jump out and save it, but the referee calls it back, they have to do it again," she told *Sports Illustrated*.[2] Scurry further justified her action to the

Los Angeles Times: "Everybody does it. It's only cheating if you get caught."[3] But even more upsetting is our society's willingness to celebrate the victory, look the other way, and ask: "What's the big deal?" Yes, we live in a culture where the end does justify the means.

> "Everybody does it. It's only cheating if you get caught."

I'm not singling out Briana Scurry to pick on her. She isn't alone. Her action, her justification, and our response are just one collective example of something bigger that's made its way into every corner of our culture. Our kids don't have to look at their World Cup heroes to get the message that "everybody's doing it, and it's only cheating if you get caught." Cheating is everywhere.

I recently read of a man named John Watson, who has launched a business venture, based in Scotland, capitalizing on cheating. His business, Ace Alibi, provides cover-up stories and services for spouses who want to pursue adulterous relationships without getting caught. For twenty-five dollars and up, Ace Alibi will help you cheat "successfully" by taking your calls, issuing fake receipts, and mailing you invitations to nonexistent social and sporting events. Watson says he's doing this to keep families together: "I simply don't believe a family should be destroyed over two or three nights of madness. If someone uses this service, they obviously want to preserve their family."[4]

Other businesses exist to "help" students get through school. For a mere ten dollars, students can secure a copy of *Cheating 101: The Benefits and Fundamentals of Earning the Easy A*.[5] The World Wide Web has sites where students can find and purchase term papers and essays on just about any topic imaginable. Two of the most popular sites are The Evil House of Cheat and School Sucks. When my own sixteen-year-old daughter was reading Charlotte Brontë's *Jane Eyre*, I went on the Web and in minutes found an online store in which papers are written for you. Of course, I never let Caitlin in on the secret, but there were twenty different papers for sale at $8.95 a page.

> ## Two of the most popular sites are The Evil House of Cheat and School Sucks.

Recent studies indicate that we are, in fact, raising a nation of cheaters. A 1998 survey of almost twenty-one thousand students by the Josephson Institute of Ethics found that 70 percent of high school students and 54 percent of middle school students admitted to cheating in the previous twelve months—an increase of 6 percent over the 1996 survey. Some think that cheating is only limited to those students struggling to get through school by the skin of their teeth. Not so. The annual *Who's Who Among American High School Students* survey of the nation's best and brightest sixteen-to-eighteen-year-olds revealed even more alarming results: 80 percent of our nation's top students admitted to cheating!

When they get to college, it's estimated by The Center for Academic Integrity, at least 75 percent of students will resort to cheating on tests.[6] Cheating has gotten so bad on college campuses that professors are using an online software product called Plagiarism.org to electronically check students' papers. During a study of the product's effectiveness, forty-five plagiarized papers were filtered

Opie Doesn't Live Here Anymore

from the three hundred submitted by students in one university science class.

Other reports find that students at all levels are going high-tech to cheat, using hidden cameras, programmed calculators, pagers, and infrared electronic schedulers. But one of the most alarming reports on cheating comes out of the New York City School District, where fifty-two educators—including some principals—provided their elementary school students with answers and help on a standardized test, all in an effort to boost scores and make their school appear more successful. [7]

How is it that our society's collective heart is marked by a culture that accepts behavior that the dictionary defines with the words *deceive, defraud, violate, mislead, dupe,* and *delude?* And why are our emerging generations so quick to assimilate cheating into their lives with little or no thought?

While the reasons are many and complex, a few stand out from the rest. First, they've lived with and watched the examples of adult cheaters. For some, they've grown up in homes where Mom and Dad cut ethical corners on "the little things." For others, life in our media-saturated world means that they can't help but see leaders, heroes, and role models who stretch the truth or engage in deception—usually without conscience or consequence.

Second, kids are growing up in a world where matters of right and wrong are determined personally on a case-by-case basis. If it "makes me feel good" or "get ahead," then it's "right." This ethical climate is perfect for growing new rules of morality, where the chasm is growing wider between what we say we believe with our lips and what we show we believe through our actions.

Of those *Who's Who* kids—80 percent of whom admitted to cheating—87 percent of that group believe "honesty is the best policy" and 75 percent say it is "always wrong" to cheat on an exam. But those same students say the number one reason students cheat is because "it doesn't seem like a big deal."

> If it "makes me feel good" or "get ahead," then it's "right." This ethical climate is perfect for growing new rules of morality.

Researcher George Barna has analyzed teen beliefs and behaviors for years. He's found that while teenagers respect integrity in other people, they aren't willing to make the sacrifices necessary to develop integrity in their own lives. Barna has found that "in many instances, integrity is taken to mean doing whatever furthers one's personal advantage without being caught."[8] Barna discovered these findings hold true for Christian and non-Christian kids alike.

In his book *Educating for Character*, Thomas Lickona relates how the folks at Random House realized the enormity of this chasm when they were preparing to publish *Telling Right from Wrong*, a book on ethics and everyday life. Random House changed their plans after they received a personal letter of high praise for the book from the chairman of Harvard University's Department of Philosophy . . . or so they thought. The problem: the book's author had forged the letter. Instead of being apologetic, he defended his action as "vigorous gamesmanship."[9]

And finally, kids say cheating is unavoidable and even necessary in a world where the pressure to succeed is enough to make them crack. Too many are growing up

Opie Doesn't Live Here Anymore

in homes where they perceive their value and worth in Mom's and Dad's eyes hinges on the grades they bring home from school. Competition for grades, the race to get into a good college, pressure from instructors, a large workload, and juggling a heavy schedule of activities all figure into the picture as well. In this kind of world, cheating is incredibly easy to justify and very difficult to resist. Yale University's Stephen Carter, author of a book on integrity, says that "we adults are establishing a climate in which we show through our behavior and through what we emphasize that the thing that matters most is me, myself, (and) getting ahead. . . . What they (our children) learn is that the key to being a successful adult is making sure that nothing like a mere law or moral principle gets in the way of getting what they want." [10]

Kids say cheating is unavoidable and even necessary in a world where the pressure to succeed is enough to make them crack.

As parents, pastors, youth workers, and educators, we can play a powerful role in leading our kids and our culture back to godly standards, where any kind of cheating or deception is seen as nothing less than wrong. Our words and example can and must combine to send a loud statement affirming this timeless and unchanging truth. That's a message we need to repeat over and over in our world today.

When we were kids playing backyard baseball or shooting baskets in the driveway, our games were often interrupted with arguments over accusations of cheating.

I can remember many times when the accused would get his way, then go on to miss a shot, strike out, or lose the game. It wasn't long before the winners were chanting a taunt that I can still hear clearly: "Cheaters never prosper, cheaters never prosper, cheaters never prosper . . . "

You see, cheating is always cheating—even if you think you won't get caught.

THE LIE OF CHRISTMAS

Youthculture@today; December 2002

I believed it would change my life. Even though I began my impatient wait for its arrival sometime in September, it usually arrived in our mailbox at 1162 Beverly Road a few weeks before Thanksgiving. Its shiny, full-color pages consumed my thoughts and attention for weeks. I ignored the first two-thirds of the book. Those pages were covered with boring pictures of clothing, tools, artificial Christmas trees, and a potpourri of boxed holiday fruits, candies, and nuts.

But for me, the true glory land was contained in the back third of the book—those pages that quickly became tattered and worn from constant perusal by me and my two very wishful younger brothers. That back third was where we would spend our time drooling over page after page of the latest in games and toys.

If you were a child in the '60s or '70s, my story is probably similar to yours. I would sit with that book for hours, using my signature colored pen (keyed for my parents as "Green=Walt") to circle anything and everything that I'd like to find under the family tree on Christmas morning. During my younger years, I wielded my pen with reckless abandon. As I got older, I would sit under my covers with a flashlight and the catalog, secretly breaking curfew while ranking my material desires numerically and calculating prices while wondering just what "Santa" might be able to afford that year. The fruit of my labors was a neatly written and ranked list to pass on to my parents.

And if you had siblings, the Sears, Roebuck and Co. Christmas catalog—a.k.a. "The Wish Book"—was the source of numerous family fights. The fights weren't just over who got to study the book and when, but why three selfish kids from the same family couldn't circle the same item with their respective colored pens. If my brothers wouldn't comply when I tried to pull rank based on seniority, I would hijack their pens and alter their wish list by going to the first two-thirds of the book and secretly circling an itchy shirt or some other article of clothing that, if it appeared under the tree, would ruin their Christmas and force them to mumble a disappointed thanks on the big morning.

And if you had siblings, the Sears, Roebuck and Co. Christmas catalog—a.k.a. "The Wish Book"— was the source of numerous family fights.

Then came the night before the day that would change my life. If there ever was a time when my mind was totally sidetracked during a worship service, it had to be Christmas Eve. All I could think about—besides "When are we going to sing the last hymn?"—was toys, toys, and more toys. I can still remember the excitement of getting home, ripping off my Sunday clothes, and slipping on my pajamas. We'd stay up later than usual running the HO trains, sipping on nonalcoholic eggnog, eating my Aunt's famous Christmas cookies, snarfing down chocolates from a Whitman's Sampler, and chewing on a piece of one of the many fruitcakes bestowed upon my pastor-father from his grateful parishioners. The only thing in our house thicker than those fruitcakes was the excitement of three little boys.

> We began our trek down the steps to the living room. The descent was always somewhat hairy as the three of us were blinded by the moose antler-sized rack of heat-radiating spotlights on top of my dad's movie camera.

Bedtime arrived—which was only a signal for us to take our excitement and move it from a vertical to a horizontal position. There were never any sugarplums dancing in my bedded head on Christmas Eve. Instead, my eyes remained as wide as saucers for what seemed like an eternity. And when sleep finally came, my anxious conscious thoughts of what I'd find under the tree soon yielded to unconscious dreams of the same stuff. Those wishful thoughts and dreams that had consumed me for weeks could be summed up in one thought: *Tomorrow morning, my life will be complete.*

At my house, we were usually up long before the sun on Christmas morning. It was my mom's responsibility to repeatedly tell us to "Wait at the top of the stairs!" while my dad took what seemed like forever to set up his 8mm movie camera while shouting "Not yet!" over and over in response to our endless, impatient shouts of "CAN WE COME DOWN NOW?!" When the words "OK, now!"

were finally spoken, we began our trek down the steps to the living room. The descent was always somewhat hairy as the three of us were blinded by the moose antler-sized rack of heat-radiating spotlights on top of my dad's movie camera. But once we reached the bottom of the steps and our eyes adjusted, we beheld the promised land right there under the Christmas tree.

Just as I remember those excited feelings of pre-Christmas anticipation, I also remember the empty and disappointed emotions I felt in the minutes and days after all the wrapping paper had been ripped off and thrown away. Don't get me wrong. I was happy—but only for a while. Some of the stuff under the tree just didn't look or work like it had in the Sears catalog or on the television commercial. Other gifts broke. And it wasn't long before the novelty wore off and everything wound up in the back of my closet or bottom of my toy box. I had believed, in my childhood naïveté, that all that stuff under the tree would somehow make me feel better, make me happy, and make me complete. It was nothing but a lie. But, stupid me . . . each and every year it was the same thing, as my yearning for completeness, peace, and satisfaction led me to buy into the great lie of Christmas one more time.

> Even though I know better, I sometimes still find myself unknowingly falling back into those same old patterns. You'd think I would have learned by now.

Even though I know better, I sometimes still find myself unknowingly falling back into those same old patterns. You'd think I would have learned by now. Maybe it's not the stuff that appears under the Christmas tree. We don't even get a Sears Christmas catalog anymore. Now it's any of a number of attractive lies floating around the cultural air we all breath that are full of nothing but empty promises. Yes, the lie of Christmas lives on strong in our culture, year-round.

> The gnawing desire to fill Pascal's God-shaped vacuum isn't limited to kids at Christmas. It's a daily battle for all people, of all ages, in all places in today's culture.

Eleventh-century Christian philosopher and theologian Anselm of Canterbury prayed about the lie of Christmas about a thousand years before I was born: *Lord, give me what you have made me want. I praise and thank you for the desire that you have inspired; perfect what you have begun, and grant me what you have made me long for.* Anselm knew that the longings and desires we all experience originate in God and can only be filled by him. He had discovered the only truth that can satisfy the hunger we all try to fill with the lie.

Six hundred years later, French philosopher Blaise Pascal pondered the same thing:

> What else does this longing and helplessness proclaim, but that there was once in each person a true happiness, of which all that now remains is the empty print and trace? We try to fill this in vain with everything around us, seeking in things that are not there the help we cannot find in those that are there. Yet none can change things, because this infinite abyss can only be filled with something that is infinite and unchanging—in other words, by God himself. God alone is our true good.

Opie Doesn't Live Here Anymore

The gnawing desire to fill Pascal's God-shaped vacuum isn't limited to kids at Christmas. It's a daily battle for all people, of all ages, in all places in today's culture. On a recent trip to Barnes & Noble, the cover of the November issue of a men's magazine caught my eye. This "10th Anniversary Special" edition of the magazine promised readers the same thing I longed for at Christmas. Inside I found "the list of a lifetime—the sixty things every man must do at least once." The article promised male readers that by experiencing everything on this definitive list they would wind up living a life that's fulfilled, peaceful, and complete. In fact, it proclaimed, "It could be the last to-do list you'll ever need." After reading it, I realized I'm only batting a measly, less-than-manly .150 and, therefore, pretty far off from experiencing complete fulfillment. The nine listed things I've done in my lifetime include owning a dog, watching your child arrive (truly amazing!), riding a motorcycle, acting like a kid (something some say I'm pretty consistent and good at!), building something, and planting a tree.

> **Apparently I'll be a miserable and unfulfilled failure until I do the fifty-one other things on the list.**

Apparently I'll be a miserable and unfulfilled failure until I do the fifty-one other things on the list, including living like a king (renting a $6,500-a-night suite in a Hong Kong hotel), reveling in the "raw sensuality" of Rio's Carnival, wrestling a bear, climbing Kilimanjaro, and experiencing sex with two women at once. Yes, the great lie of Christmas lives on in today's culture. We believe we can fill the gnawing hunger with anything and everything but the one right thing. What a lie!

Without a doubt, the greatest inheritance we can pass on to the kids we know and love is the truth about the lie. Not only that the lie of Christmas is a lie, but that the truth of Christmas is the truth. My parents passed on that truth in many ways. But as I think back on my memories of childhood Christmases past, it was their Christmas lists that told the truth so clearly. Every year, when I would take a break from my selfishness to ask them what they wanted for Christmas, the answer was always the same: "We don't need anything." Then, when Christmas morning arrived, I would feel so bad for them as they opened boxes of socks, sweaters, tools, kitchenware, and itchy shirts—all stuff from the first two-thirds of "The Wish Book." Much to my surprise, they were never disappointed. Why? Because they had already been satisfied by the truth of Christmas. They had embraced the gift of the baby whose birthday we were celebrating. Sure, my parents thought Christmas gifts were nice and they appreciated every one of them. But the hole in their souls had already been filled. Because they didn't want anything, I quickly learned they already had everything.

> The hole in their souls had already been filled.
> Because they didn't want anything,
> I quickly learned they already had everything.

Shortly after Pascal died, someone found a piece of paper sewn into the lining of his jacket. Pascal had placed it there as a constant reminder of what "the truth of Christmas" had meant to him when he first believed and experienced it. On the paper were recorded the words he had written when the God-shaped vacuum of his life had been filled by the baby Jesus: "From about half past ten in the evening to about half an hour after midnight. Fire. God of Abraham, God of Isaac, God of Jacob. Not the God of philosophers and scholars. Absolute certainty. Beyond reasons. Joy. Peace. Forgetfulness of the world and everything but God. The world has not known thee, but I have known thee. Joy! Joy! Joy! Tears of joy!"

The old man Simeon waited in great expectation for the arrival of the promised Messiah. He knew what it was he longed for. The Holy Spirit had shown him that, before he died, he would see the Christ child. Eight days after the birth of the baby Jesus, Simeon held the truth of Christmas in his arms and praised God with these words: "God, you can now release your servant; release me in peace as you promised. With my own eyes I've seen your salvation. It's now out in the open for everyone to see" (Luke 2:29-31, *The Message*). While the lie of Christmas lives on strong, it can't compare to the life-changing power of what Christmas is really about. This truth of Christmas is the very thing—the only thing—that answers our deepest longings and fills the most empty of lives!

THOUGHTS ON THE VMAS

Blog; September 1, 2006

As promised, I took the time to watch the Video Music Awards last night . . . a show that, by the way, was so flat I had to force myself to hang in for the entire three-plus hours. (It all began with a feeble performance by Justin Timberlake, the pop star who's desperately trying to attain staying power by reinventing himself over and over again. He had trouble singing on key, which made it a painful performance to watch.) Still, the annual production continues to serve as a window into a changing culture—a window that can be a valuable one—for those who follow Christ and want to love and lead kids to do the same. Even though it's sometimes difficult to do, we need to look and keep on looking. If you're like me, you probably had an emotional reaction both during and after the show. For me, it was a sense of deep heartache for a world that wears its hunger for redemption on its sleeve—while grabbing for the brass ring in all the wrong places. What follows are some random thoughts I jotted down while tuned in.

> For me, it was a sense of deep heartache for a world that wears its hunger for redemption on its sleeve— while grabbing for the brass ring in all the wrong places.

The crowd was largely void of energy, detached. The biggest applause came in response to the two oldest guys on the show. When Lou Reed implored MTV to return to its rock 'n' roll roots, the crowd agreed, providing more evidence that the music world is flat, that the lack of creativity in hip-hop and pop has left us bored, and that the pervasiveness of media has made everything so familiar that we appear tuned in . . . but we're being lulled to sleep as the same old stuff is trotted out over and over.

Old guy Al Gore probably embarrassed his kids with his efforts to connect with the crowd through humor, but his environmental message was one the audience seemed to embrace and applaud. (As an aside, I know too many

Christians who think that anything to do with Al Gore and/or environmentalism has to be part of some liberal conspiracy. We desperately need to get over it. God's creation mandate to be stewards of his world should have had us trumpeting the environmental message a long, long time ago.)

What were impressionable young viewers told was important? The overall flavor of the show conveyed that ego and attitude are everywhere. Humility is absent. Traditional virtues have been shoved aside. Rather, life is about freedom of expression, whether that be sexually, through profanity, by objectifying women and acting on that objectification, or through the accumulation of stuff. We're encouraged to indulge our lusts. There's obviously a hole in the soul. If the popular music culture is pointing to a redeemer, that redeemer is found in twisted forms of the God-created and God-given gift of sexuality.

> The overall flavor of the show conveyed that ego and attitude are everywhere. Humility is absent. Traditional virtues have been shoved aside. Rather, life is about freedom of expression.

The show also clearly reflected several cultural realities. Our kids are the consummate media-saturated and media-savvy multitaskers. Not only could they watch the show, they could log on to the VMA Web site to see dozens of uncensored, hidden camera views. The reality of multiculturalism was evident in big ways. The success of youth marketing and evidence of rapidly expanding media options could be seen in the addition of a new award this year: Ringtone of the Year.

And strutting their stuff onstage were three poster girls for current cultural realities that should make us ache for kids. The painfully thin Nicole Richie reminds us of the battle so many are fighting against eating disorders, an issue fueled by the same media that made Nicole Richie popular in the first place. Paris Hilton—the poster girl for do-nothing but be-everything celebrity—reminds us of the need to point our kids to positive and godly role models. And then there is Jessica Simpson. It seems that year after year I wind up mentioning her and her ongoing crusade to consistently promote an inconsistent and dis-integrated faith. She represents so much that is wrong with the church, the way we do evangelism, the type of faith we call people to, and our unwillingness to follow Christ everywhere, in everything. And of course, she encourages our girls to be nothing more than their physical selves. As I watched her onstage last night, I couldn't help but think about the story I heard in the media this week, that she's been recently linked to John Mayer. Did you know one of his hit songs is "Your Body Is a Wonderland"? Then I think about Jessica's pastor-dad, Joe, and the role he's played in shaping the Jessica Simpson brand. Think about that the next time you hear the lyrics to Mayer's song "Daughters." All three of these women and the realities they represent should shape our parenting and ministries.

> **Music and its visuals shape our culture and our kids' worldviews.**

One of the highlights, for me, was Kanye West's introduction of the Video Vanguard Award, which went to video maker Hype Williams. It included some great

Opie Doesn't Live Here Anymore

commentary on the power of music and music video. I agree with Kanye here: music and its visuals shape our culture and our kids' worldviews.

And because I always get tired of artists "thanking God" and the confusion that it breeds among our Christian kids as to who God is and the shape of Christian faith, I actually liked what the guy from Avenge Sevenfold said when his band received the Best New Artist Award: "I'd like to thank God—whichever one I believe in."

Finally, I couldn't help but shake my head and hurt deeply over one of MTV's animated network promos, this one featuring a mouse humping the MTV logo. Most kids would laugh at it and tell me I'm hopelessly old-fashioned and out-of-date for being concerned about an innocent little cartoon. But I viewed it after flipping around to other networks during some of the VMA commercial breaks. One flip took me to the Travel Channel and a special on Florida's best beaches. I happened to tune in while they were featuring Panama City and its reputation as a spring break destination. One woman they interviewed—who may have been with the tourist bureau—said this about Panama City's spring-breakers: "They're here to lose all inhibitions and leave their morals at the door."

That makes me ache inside. After watching last night's VMAs, I wonder if our culture is slowly moving into a state of perpetual spring break.

How to respond to such emptiness? It's important to take these short glimpses into our culture. If we are followers of Christ who continue to pursue him and, as a result, have truth coursing through our veins, we're able to enter into this world with eyes of faith that allow us to discern error from truth—and keep us from assimilating error into our lives.

In addition, followers of Christ will look at how fallenness expresses itself in our culture, not with eyes that condemn, but with eyes that weep with God over the depth of depravity and lostness—especially in the lives of those who are young and impressionable.

Life Lessons from Mr. Thome

Blog; February 24, 2005

Yesterday I had the opportunity to experience one of those amazing, teachable moments with my twelve-year-old son, Nate. I'm speaking here in Orlando and he came along for the trip. We've had some wonderful times together this week, but it'll be difficult to beat the excitement we shared yesterday.

On the spur of the moment I asked Nate if he'd like to take the drive over to Clearwater to visit the spring training home of the Philadelphia Phillies. He thought that'd be fun so we hopped in the car and arrived at the Carpenter Complex around noon. The forty-man Phillies roster was split up on the four practice fields getting ready for batting practice. We found Jim Thome and a couple of the team's other big guns and ran out to position ourselves beyond the left field fence in the hope of scoring a home run ball or two. Our competition included a hodgepodge of collectors who had been there all morning nabbing balls and filling their backpacks. I'll spare you the details, but we wound up grabbing six balls in a half hour. Seeing the excitement on Nate's face was like watching a Norman Rockwell painting come to life.

Opie Doesn't Live Here Anymore

After the team cleared the field and headed to the locker room, one of the parking lot attendants told us where we could go to try to get a player autograph or two. We went and positioned ourselves with about fifteen others at a fence bordering the players' parking lot. The lot was filled with two types of cars—the kind most of us would drive, and then an ostentatious collection of Hummers and a couple of European sports cars you'd expect millionaire athletes to be sporting.

> "You know me better than that.
> You'll never see me driving one of those!
> That's not who I am."

One by one the players left the locker room. Nate waited patiently and wound up getting our half-dozen balls signed by fourteen of the Phillies' players. But the best moment came when Thome walked to the fence. We knew he was coming our way since his family-style Chevy Suburban—nothing fancy about this one—was parked nearby. Nate had purchased a mini Phillies bat and marker that he was saving in case Thome stopped to sign. Just as the fans at the fence were starting to focus on Thome, one of his well-known teammates was climbing into a fancy yellow Ferrari equipped with some wild-looking doors. Attention flip-flopped back and forth between the two. One of the fans at the fence yelled out to Thome, "Hey Jim, when are you going to get one of those cars to drive?!" Thome started laughing, then looked at us and said, "Come on now, you know me better than that. You'll never see me driving one of those!" The guy yelled back, "Why? Because you won't fit in it?" "No," Thome answered. "Because that's not who I am."

If you know anything at all about Thome, you know he's a pretty level-headed, down-to-earth guy who hasn't allowed his fame and fortune to get to his head—or his heart. He politely signed Nate's bat (along with everything else people put in front of him) and then climbed into his car to drive away. As we got into our car to leave, I was able to seize the moment and discuss the life lessons we had just seen—including the amazing contrast between the values of two famous baseball players—and how one set of values reflect the way and will of Jesus.

Several times during the drive back to Orlando, I looked over at Nate happily holding his autographed bat and balls. He had come home with more than some nice souvenirs. He was also carrying a lesson I hope he'll treasure even more—and live—for the rest of his life.

WHOSE GOD IS IT, ANYWAY?

Youthculture@today; December 1999

Thomas, Seann, and Chris speak about their faith in terms that would make any youth worker or Christian parent proud. Eighteen-year-old Thomas Ian Nicholas attends a Bible study and plays in a Christian band. He writes his music "with God," "for God," and "about God." Seann William Scott, also eighteen, says his family "lived for our trust in God; even in junior high people used to call me 'church boy.'" The third member of the trio, Chris Klein, isn't afraid to tell people that he too is a Christian.[11]

You'd probably assume that Thomas, Seann, and Chris, like all Christian teens and adults, wage the daily battle to obey God and conform to his will while being faced with the constant barrage of temptations thrown at them by today's culture—from time to time they might even mess up. Consequently, you might not be surprised at the trio's attraction to last summer's sexually charged teen blockbuster comedy, *American Pie*, a film about four average high school guys who face the dilemma of losing their virginity by making a pact to "get laid" during the three weeks remaining before their prom.

> **More alarming is that none of the three saw any inconsistency between following God and taking lead roles in the movie.**

What should surprise you about the trio's attraction to the film is not that they would pay to go see *American Pie*, but that Thomas, Seann, and Chris were paid to star in the film. Even more alarming is that none of the three saw any inconsistency between following God and taking lead roles in the movie. Sadly, it's a film that "treats" its young audience to an extreme dose of in-your-face immorality (intercourse, oral sex, masturbation, etc.), including one of the film's main characters masturbating into a hot apple pie.

Welcome to youth culture at the dawn of the new millennium—a crude and confusing world in which an increasing amount of consistent spiritual inconsistency and glaring contradiction socks committed Christian parents and youth workers right in their stomachs, while the same things roll unnoticed off our kids' backs. It's a world where those who lovingly challenge immorality and sin may get a "So what?" response, even from kids who profess to follow the narrow road that leads to life.

Known as millennial kids, the generation of young people born after 1980 are more diverse and pluralistic than any generation before. As children raised in the Information Age, they're growing up surrounded by an unprecedented rate of change in both society and youth culture. Their place as the second generation steeped in the postmodern worldview has led to their collective soul regarding truth as relative. At the level of adopting moral and religious belief, this shift leads to the individual "freedom" of every man choosing for himself. Decisions are made not on universally acknowledged and transcendent standards of right and wrong, but on a person's own feelings at any given point in time. Emotion takes precedence over reason. In a world like this, there's nothing wrong with three Christian teens inviting millions of their peers to sit in a dark theater and watch as they celebrate and indulge their sexuality in a feature-length film.

> In a world like this, there's nothing wrong with three Christian teens inviting millions of their peers to sit in a dark theater and watch as they celebrate and indulge their sexuality in a feature-length film.

Like it or not, this is our world. Shaking our heads or wagging a scolding finger won't make it go away. Rather, we've got to deeply understand and gracefully respond if we want to see young hearts and minds turn from sin to embrace the truth. In the quest to understand, we need to answer two questions: What do we know about the spiritual heartbeat pulsating in today's millennial youth culture? And, what are the distinctive marks of millennial faith?

Opie Doesn't Live Here Anymore

Everywhere you look, smorgasbord spirituality is looking back. From MTV to magazines to television to film to advertising—there's not a corner of popular culture that isn't wearing spirituality on its sleeve. The God-shaped vacuum in today's children and teens has led to a deep and conscious interest in spiritual things. A recent *USA Weekend* survey on teens and self-image found that students cite "religion" as the second-strongest influence in their lives, outranked only by parents, and ahead of teachers, peers, boyfriends, girlfriends, and the media. But like the constantly reinvented and unconventional spirituality of pop star Madonna, their religion is composed of an ever-changing combination of elements unique to each individual. This smorgasbord of spirituality is much like a restaurant close to my home that advertises a "140-foot-long buffet of mouth-watering food." Each and every day, busloads of ravenous folks arrive to load their plates and eat their fill. With so much to choose from, everyone creates their distinct combination based on what personally appeals to their taste buds at that moment in time. During the feeding frenzy, no two plates are ever identical.

> **The God-shaped vacuum in today's children and teens has led to a deep and conscious interest in spiritual things.**

The same diversity marks the spiritual plates of today's youth culture. In his book *Virtual Faith*, Thomas Beaudoin says that young people are "taking religion into their own hands."[12] At the same time, consistent, biblical Christianity is seen as outdated, irrelevant, judgmental, and obnoxiously exclusive. The result is personalized combinations merging bits and pieces of different faith traditions—Christianity, paganism, pragmatism, Wicca, mysticism, Eastern religions, the occult, and more—all from the spiritual buffet table. It's truly a "whatever" spirituality.

And while God is mentioned all the time, don't believe that "God" is necessarily God. The summer 1999 "Hot List" issue of *Rolling Stone* magazine reported that the "Hot Image Makeover" of the year belongs to God: "No, No, No, God isn't dead: he's just being re-branded."[13] Judging from what I've seen and heard on the music award shows for the last ten years, God's been a big part of the success of the popular music industry's hottest chart-topping acts. More often than not, the acceptance speech begins with the trophy-holder looking heavenward and thanking "God" or "My Lord and Savior Jesus Christ" for "giving me the ability" and/or "making this possible." But their own stage performances, song lyrics, videos, and off-stage antics usually leave me scratching my head and asking: "What God are they talking about?"

> **Don't be mistaken: "God talk" isn't always a reference to the God of the Bible. It's usually a rebranded God.**

Don't be mistaken: "God talk" isn't always a reference to the God of the Bible. It's usually a rebranded God. In today's world, God is recreated by and for the eyes of the beholder. One recent survey of teens found that 94 percent believe in God. The next question should have been: "Who or what is the God you believe in?" Researcher George Barna has discovered that "to a growing number of teens, the name (or description) 'God' is an elastic expression: it can be stretched to cover just about anything you want

Opie Doesn't Live Here Anymore

it to imply. When teens talk about God, they may be alluding to a unique and holy being, a genteel universal spirit, or an amorphous and impersonal higher power."[14]

> **The article presented Spears as a refreshingly innocent new face in popular culture who "cleaves" to her Christian faith, prays daily, and finds the TV show *South Park* to be "sacrilegious."**

And sadly, faith and life might never intersect. Shortly after sixteen-year-old sensation Britney Spears hit the charts, *Rolling Stone* ran an article (April 15, 1999) titled "Britney Spears: Inside the Heart and Mind and Bedroom of America's New Teen Queen." The article presented Spears as a refreshingly innocent new face in popular culture who "cleaves" to her Christian faith, prays daily, and finds the TV show *South Park* to be "sacrilegious."[15] But then I saw the article's four full-page photos of Spears—seductively dressed in sexually suggestive poses. Inconsistent and troubling—but not unusual. It's more evidence of what our casual observations continue to show: that verbalized faith, even when biblical and orthodox, doesn't always translate into real life.

Of course, this is nothing new. When I was a college student, I attended a conference in which the late Tom Skinner challenged us as young Christians to integrate our faith into all of life. As part of his challenge, he shared an interesting statistic: "Fifty million Americans say that they are born-again Christians." Then, after a long pause, Skinner asked this question: "If that's true, where are they?" While the chasm between verbalized assent to faith and testimony to faith through lifestyle has always been wide, it's growing wider. No doubt, the consistently inconsistent example of those of us who are older has done little or nothing to turn the tide.

> These kids are a breath of fresh air and great to be around. How can we answer their spiritual hunger with the unchanging Truth that satisfies once and for all?

The confused spirituality of the millennial generation presents the church with a unique—and yet exciting—challenge. The millennials' skepticism about Christianity is discouraging, but at the same time they have a very real enthusiasm and willingness to engage in deep conversations about spiritual matters. These kids are a breath of fresh air and great to be around. How can we answer their spiritual hunger with the unchanging Truth that satisfies once and for all? While not exhaustive, here are four initial steps we've got to take if we are serious about pointing them to a serious commitment to know, love, and serve the one true God.

First, we've got to take a long, hard look in the mirror. The millennial generation has done the church a valuable service by criticizing our hypocrisy and inconsistency. More often than not, their observations are accurate. It's time to admit that we're guilty of preaching, usually through example, a false "God." For starters, why should we get upset about young Christians who sinfully pursue starring roles in *American Pie* when we ourselves preach Christ while eagerly engaging in the sinful pursuit of the American Dream? After all, we've taught them well.

Second, we've got to be sure that our "God" is truly God; we have to be oriented correctly. When scuba divers are down deep, it's easy for them to become confused and disoriented. Since water diffuses light, divers often find themselves surrounded by illumination, making it difficult to discern which way is up. Feeling weightless and without a sense of gravity contributes to this confusion. The only way to distinguish up from down is to watch the direction in which the air bubbles travel. Divers who lose their sense of direction risk drowning if they trust their inner senses more than those bubbles. They are taught early on that no matter how they feel, no matter what they think, their bubbles are always right. In a day and age in which "God" is recreated and redefined, and so many are left spiritually confused and disoriented, we've got to be constantly checking our spiritual air bubbles. Which way is truly up? Which way is God? There's no substitute for faithful pursuit of the one true God through time spent studying God's self-revelation in the Bible.

> **Gone are the days where reaching kids through youth ministry is simply a matter of "if you build it (a big program) they will come (into the church)."**

Third, we must go. Today's rapidly changing youth culture requires that we see the world of the millennial generation as a foreign mission field. They are thinking, believing, and acting in ways that are increasingly different from how we do the same things. We must know them, understand their world, and walk with them in it. Gone are the days where reaching kids through youth ministry is simply a matter of "if you build it (a big program) they will come (into the church)." The voice we must hear and obey is the voice of Jesus as he says to us, "Go into their world."

And finally, we've got to live the truth in the context of deep, meaningful, and enduring relationships with young people. Sitting them in a room and talking at them with a barrage of well-reasoned propositional truth isn't the way to point them to the one true God. Of course, we can't deny the necessity of verbally communicating the truth; that's got to happen. What we need to do is change the context. The millennial generation will benefit most from our efforts to live the faith through relationships. Collectively, they are calling the church to "show me with your life before you tell it to me with your words." When Ugandan Archbishop Janani Luwum was challenged about his friendship with the tyrannical dictator of that country, Idi Amin (who later murdered him), he responded with a challenge that captures the importance of communicating truth through relationships: "The best way to show a stick is crooked is not to argue about it or spend time denouncing it, but to lay a straight stick alongside it."

Young men like Thomas, Seann, and Chris are terribly confused. They're part of a hungry and refreshingly enthusiastic generation that's looking for answers to their spiritual cries. It's time to walk the Truth alongside these guys and the rest of their millennial peers. It's time to get out of the way and let God be God.

EMBRACING THE COLLISION

Your word is a lamp to my feet and a light for my path.
(Psalm 119:105)

Now fear the Lord and serve him with all faithfulness. Throw away the gods your forefathers worshiped beyond the River and in Egypt, and serve the Lord. But if serving the Lord seems undesirable to you, then choose for yourselves this day whom you will serve, whether the gods your forefathers served beyond the River, or the god of the Amorites, in whose land you are living. But as for me and my household, we will serve the Lord. (Joshua 24:14, 15)

I am the way and the truth and the life. No one comes to the Father except through me. (John 14:6)

1. WHY DO WE OFTEN WEAR A SPIRITUAL BLINDFOLD that is both attractive and convincing? Why is it difficult to see the world the way it truly is?

2. KIDS OFTEN SAY THAT CHEATING IS UNAVOIDABLE— and even necessary—in a world where the pressure to succeed is so great. Reflect on your own life. Do you put extra pressure on your kids? How can you help them deal with the pressure they'll receive from multiple people and situations in life?

3. "FOLLOWERS OF CHRIST WILL LOOK AT HOW FALLENNESS EXPRESSES ITSELF IN OUR CULTURE, not with eyes that condemn, but with eyes that weep with God over the depth of depravity and lostness, especially in the lives of those who are young and impressionable" (from my blog "Thoughts on the VMAs"). Is this the way you view youth culture? Why is this often difficult?

4. WHY DO YOU THINK THE CONFUSED SPIRITUALITY OF THE MILLENNIAL GENERATION presents the church with a unique—and yet exciting—challenge? What can you do on a personal, church, and community level to meet this challenge?

Opie Doesn't Live Here Anymore

RETHINKING:
HOW WE DO
CHRISTIANITY

SOMEWHERE ALONG THE WAY WE GOT LOST ... twice. The first time it led to our separation from God. The way humanity has chosen to live life since the time we first wandered away might best be summed up in the Frank Sinatra classic "My Way." But thankfully, God didn't leave us there.

Reading the Scriptures from beginning to end offers plenty of evidence that those who, like me, have been chosen and rescued by God—after getting lost the first time—are prone to wander off the path to disobediently do their own thing again and again and again. The nation of Israel wound up wandering in the desert for forty years because of its insistence on doing things its own way. God used judges and prophets to set his people back on course when they'd choose to follow their own way.

The Son of God himself, who came to earth to provide the way back to God, spent much of his time here instructing the rescued about the very real temptations they would face because of their inclination to follow their sinful natures. And most of the New Testament letters were written to get the church back on course after it wandered into a faulty or imbalanced way of doing things.

I used to read these accounts and wonder how people could be so stupid as to do their own thing. Then I came to realize that my wondering stopped every time I saw the answer looking at me in my mirror. There's nothing in these chapters of the divine drama that I haven't experienced for myself. I was lost, but have been rescued. Still, even though you'd think I'd get it by now, Sinatra's mantra has all too often become my own . . . and I wander away to here, there, and everywhere. Even though I've been found for eternity, I allow the distractions and temptations of life to lead me away from my heavenly Father, much like a curious and

Opie Doesn't Live Here Anymore

easily enticed child—otherwise safe in his parents' care—who wanders away from those same parents at the mall. I've found that I constantly need to take a look in the mirror to ask myself: "Am I doing things my way, or God's way?"

> I used to read these accounts and wonder how people could be so stupid as to do their own thing. Then I came to realize that my wondering stopped every time I saw the answer looking at me in my mirror.

These stories also are born from the ongoing struggle between who we are and who we're called to be as we live together in the company of other beggars who've chosen to eat from the Bread of Life. I've found that, as the church, we constantly need to take a look in the mirror to ask ourselves: "Are we doing things our way, or God's way?" It's my deep prayer that God will be constantly leading me (and us) to the mirror, comparing what I (we) see reflected back with the image and will of the one who secured me (us) in the first place.

THINKING ABOUT CHURCH . . .

Blog; April 4, 2006

I don't want to be a jerk. I don't want to get in the way of God's Spirit. Nor do I want to come across as divisive. But I'm concerned that verbalizing some thoughts that have been gnawing at me for some time—and the gnawing seems to be growing in frequency and depth—will leave the impression that I'm a divisive jerk who happens to like getting in the way of what God's doing. I hesitate to pass on some thoughts I've had about how some of us are doing church, but I need to. Keep in mind that I'm in process on this, prayerfully striving to be biblically faithful, and open to being convinced otherwise about these opinions if somebody's willing to help me.

The need was prompted by a note my nineteen-year-old son slid to me in the middle of worship this past Sunday. More on that in a minute. It's no secret that I attend a rather traditional church. While our church is traditional in liturgy, everything in our worship service is done with great thought and explanation. Like the unfolding divine drama, our service unfolds with beauty and deep meaning—from our prayers, to our recitations of creeds, to the preparatory quiet of our sanctuary, to our use of the great hymns of the faith, to our confessions, to our sung responses, to our celebration of the Lord's Supper, to the primacy of the Word, and so on. In the midst of the quiet and the tradition, God speaks loudly to me. When he speaks, it is with a depth that challenges me and forces me to go deeper with him and his Word.

At times, my emotions are moved. At other times, they're not. If the familiar components of our services

Opie Doesn't Live Here Anymore

that I encounter week after week become dull and boring, I take full blame. Each of those components are there because I, in my humanness, need to be reminded of who I am, who God is, what I believe, and what he's done for me. If I'm focusing on that, I can't help but be moved.

> Somehow the emphasis on *me* and *I* leaves the impression that we believe worship is for us. That's wrong. Again, we're the performers and God is the audience.

Perhaps the biggest worship mistake I'm prone to fall into is the fallacy of believing that when I arrive and take my seat, it's time for me to be entertained. That's not what corporate worship is. Rather, I'm the performer and God's the audience. Worship that gets that right is the only kind of corporate worship that can be described as "good." All too often I hear adults and kids in their after-worship commentary say things like "That worship was awesome!" OK, but what do you mean by that? When I ask clarifying questions about what made worship "great" I've heard everything from "It made me feel good" to "I loved the music" to "It didn't bore me" to "I think the smoke machine was awesome." Somehow the emphasis on *me* and *I* leaves the impression that we believe worship is for us. That's wrong. Again, we're the performers and God is the audience. That's what it means to live life to the glory of God.

And I think we've also reduced our definition and understanding of worship to the one hour that we sing together each week. But the Scriptures make it clear that the most important type of worship should take place during every one of the other 167 hours in our week. If you don't believe me, just read the Old Testament's minor prophets.

Back to my son's note. It read: "After being in so many contemporary worship services, this is mentally straining." In my conversation with him after the service I realized he was not just complaining, but stating a fact. Like me, I think he wants things to be somewhat easy. He realizes that depth requires some hard work. We are to love the Lord with all our minds. For him, it's come down to a battle between being entertained and working hard.

> **Like me, I think he wants things to be somewhat easy. He realizes that depth requires some hard work. We are to love the Lord with all our minds.**

It's funny, but just the day before he handed me that note, I had picked up and read a campus newspaper. One article that caught my eye was written by a megachurch attender in response to criticisms of how corporate worship is done by many megachurches (generally accepted as those churches with an average weekend worship attendance of two thousand or more). While the article raised some very good points, it seemed to me that the author provided a weak defense of worship that's designed to be entertaining and fun. Entertaining and fun worship was justified on the grounds that Jesus never commanded us to be reserved and that the Old Testament tells us that David danced before God.

I'm not sure that argument is one that addresses the crux of the criticism—especially when the group in question is a self-described seeker-sensitive church, for people who don't go to church and who don't already have a relationship with Christ. If you're marketing the church and focusing on making people feel welcome, you're trying to reach an audience. That audience—or group of consumers—answers the ads to get something out of the experience. Should we be dumbing down and softening the radical, confrontational, offensive, counter-cultural message of the gospel to make it easier for people to accept? Don't they wind up seeing themselves as the consumer/audience in the corporate worship setting? Don't we see them as the audience when we want to entertain them and design our services to do so? Is there something wrong with followers of Christ who leave their churches to attend a more entertaining service where "the worship meets my needs"? Isn't this just a sign that our culture of easily broken commitments and quick divorce has crept into the church? Where is our commitment to our local church community in the context of knowing that no group of believers this side of Heaven will ever be perfect and devoid of problems and issues?

And I wonder . . . can and should people who don't know God really worship in a corporate setting? Can they consciously worship at all? And are we really helping them grow in their understanding of the depths and riches of God when our music tends to be frothy, shallow, simple, me-centered mantras that we more or less chant over and over . . . with the result being a dumbed-down understanding of God that focuses less on who he is and more on what I can get from him?

Could it be that this type of approach to doing church and worship is at the root of the current American faith that looks more like what Christian Smith describes as "moralistic therapeutic deism"[1] than radical, biblical Christianity? I'm all for excellence; we're called to it. But is our excellence meant to attract attention, or give glory to God?

This week I've been reading Os Guinness's book, *Unspeakable: Facing Up to Evil in an Age of Genocide and Terror*. Guinness tells a story that got me thinking about a pressing and growing problem in the church. He relates some of Primo Levi's thoughts on evil as recorded in his book *Survival in Auschwitz*: "Monsters exist, but they are too few in number to be truly dangerous. More dangerous are the common men, the functionaries ready to believe and to act without asking questions."[2] Wow. I'm wondering if we've become a church of thoughtless functionaries . . . people who jump into "doing" without first asking the necessary questions. Is that happening as we plan how we do church? If that's who we are, then we are dangerous.

> I'm all for excellence; we're called to it.
> But is our excellence meant to attract attention,
> or give glory to God?

While listening to the radio, I once heard the pastor of a large church say, "We must be doing things right. People are coming." I'm sorry, but the more I think about what he said, the more I can't believe my ears. Is that how we measure the rightness of our doing? Does successful packaging make our actions morally and biblically sound? The Rolling Stones also did something "right" on last summer's concert tour—the band's promotions drew a crowd. My local JCPenney store must be doing something

Opie Doesn't Live Here Anymore

"right"—its ads draw crowds into the store. We could go on and on in giving examples of how effective marketing draws consumers. But does *successful* equal *right* in the context of the church?

> **If I'm raising questions in your mind, if you agree with me, or even if you want to string me up right now, can I encourage you to join me on this journey of simply asking, "What is proper worship?"**

Perhaps I need to clarify again: I'm not trying to be divisive. I'm not questioning the hearts of those whose methodologies I'm struggling to understand theologically. I know many of them personally and I believe their underlying motives are good. Rather, what I'm struggling with is the wholesale selling out to an approach to ministry that may in fact compromise the radical call of Jesus.

If I'm raising questions in your mind, if you agree with me, or even if you want to string me up right now, can I encourage you to join me on this journey of simply asking, "What is proper worship?" If so, I'd love for you to read a book by Marva Dawn that I've just finished. In *Reaching Out Without Dumbing Down*, Dawn makes readers think. Ponder this quote—it's certainly turned up the heat on this growing feeling inside of me:

> Christians were horrified in 1994 when an anti-abortion protester killed two people—a doctor and his escort—in his attempt to "save lives." The irony is too obvious. How can taking lives ever be consistent with the goal of preserving them? In the same way, many churches [that] want desperately to attract people to Christ miss the point by offering worship so shallow that not enough of Christ is proclaimed to engender lasting belief.

Rethinking: How We Do Christianity

Some of you might protest that my analogy is too harsh, but I wonder if the practice of dumbing down worship isn't, in the long run, equally fatal to the faith. If people are introduced to a Christianity composed only of happiness and good feelings, where will the staying power be when chronic illness, family instability, or long-term unemployment threaten? If worship is only fun, how will those attracted to such worship have enough commitment to work on the conflicts that inevitably develop because all of us in the [c]hurch are sinful human beings?[3]

What are our options? I like the options Dawn cites as she quotes Walter Brueggemann, when he insists that the gospel must be both proclaimed and heard as:

- intellectually credible in an unreflective society;
- politically critical and constructive in a cynical community;
- morally dense and freighted in a self-indulgent society;
- artistically satisfying in a society overwhelmed by religious kitsch;
- pastorally attentive in a society of easy but fake answers.[4]

And now, to keep on thinking . . .

LESSONS FROM PETE

Youthculture@today; September 2004

I was sweaty, tired, grumpy, and I'm pretty sure I had bad breath. Judging from what I saw, heard, and smelled, everyone else was in the same condition.

That's the way it is when you climb onto an airplane at 10 PM. Not only is the thing filled with the sights, sounds, and smells of dozens of travelers who've been cultivating sweat, fatigue, impatience, and halitosis all day, just like you, but there's also that unmistakable stale odor that lingers from the hundreds of travelers who were in and

Opie Doesn't Live Here Anymore

out of the thing during the day's previous who-knows-how-many flights. To top it all off, the best the airline could do for me was put me in the dreaded window seat at the end of a three-seat row . . . which, of course, meant I was going to be sandwiched between a curved wall and someone just as smelly as me. Great. Still, it's better than being stuck in the middle.

> I managed to live out my faith through maintaining a commitment to prayer and a spirit of Christian love. How? I asked the Lord to get me from Atlanta to Dallas as quickly as possible.

While my circumstances were bad, I managed to live out my faith through maintaining a commitment to prayer and a spirit of Christian love. How? I asked the Lord to get me from Atlanta to Dallas as quickly as possible, and, "by the way, I don't want anyone sitting next to me." OK, I wasn't asking. I was telling.

I was the first one in my row to settle into my seat, which meant that I kept my eye on everyone else coming down the aisle, all the while muttering under my breath "No . . . Please, no . . . Keep going . . . Don't sit down next to me." The plane was quickly filling up and smelling worse by the minute, but God was answering my prayer. To my left sat two empty seats.

Until it happened.

"It" was the arrival of a thirty-something young man who had been assigned the seat on the aisle. It was bad, but not as bad as it could have been. He could have been seated right next to me. As he was settling into his seat the flight attendant closed the door. I counted my blessings that there would be a no-man's-land of sorts between us and that I was going to get some much-needed sleep. After all, a full day of ministry lay ahead.

I think I was right in the middle of closing my eyes when it happened again. This time "it" was my rowmate's overt expression of friendliness. "Hi, my name's Pete!" he enthusiastically said as he threw his right hand in my direction. Goodness sakes! It was ten o'clock at night! How could someone be so perky? We shook hands while I less-than-enthusiastically introduced myself. *Oh no*, I thought. *A talker.* Normally, I love chatting with people I don't know. But it was late and I was tired.

> "Hi, my name's Pete!" he enthusiastically said as he threw his right hand in my direction. Goodness sakes! It was ten o'clock at night!

As he started rooting through his bag he looked over at me and asked, "Do you like music?" Even though I was tired, he was starting to get my attention. "I love music," I replied. Pete then informed me he had just gotten a new iPod and that he had two sets of headphones. "We can listen together on the way to Dallas," Pete declared. That was a little bit odd, but intriguing. At least it would get me out of having to talk.

But then it really started to get strange with his next question: "Walt, are you a God-fearing man?" Immediately, I started talking with God again: *Oh, Lord, why do you have me sitting next to a Christian?* My brain went right into the stereotyping mode as I imagined spending the next two hours as this man's evangelistic project. I knew I'd be able to explain to Pete that I already was who he thought I wasn't, but based on past experiences with guys like him, I was going to be spending two hours defending my theology from his corrective assaults. Suddenly, I started to rattle off in my head all the reasons why I don't like Christians, even though I'm one myself.

Once I answered Pete's question in the affirmative, an amazing thing happened. Pete looked me in the eye and said, "If you are a God-fearing man, would you mind if I ask you some questions about spirituality? I'm going through a difficult time and I need some help." Because situations like this don't arise so effortlessly and easily every day—or in a lifetime, for that matter—I started to look around for the hidden cameras. I knew God wasn't answering my prayers for sleep, but the next two hours could be a pretty exciting answer to prayers I've prayed many times before. I was now fully awake.

> Suddenly, I started to rattle off in my head all the reasons why I don't like Christians, even though I'm one myself.

As I reached into my pocket for a couple of breath mints, I quietly asked the Lord to guide my conversation, and—oh yeah—to forgive me for all the other prayers I had prayed since setting foot on that plane. Into my head popped some great advice given by Francis Schaeffer for a time just like this. Schaeffer once said that if he had one hour to spend with someone he didn't know and who didn't know Christ, he would spend the first fifty-five minutes concentrating on listening and the last five minutes giving the person a biblical truth that somehow applied to what he had heard during the first fifty-five. With that advice fresh in my mind, I set out with determination to listen to Pete for the next two hours.

Time flew by as Pete told me his amazing story: He had been born in poverty in another country. When he was nine his father moved the family to the United States in hopes of a better life, but life for Pete never got better. It just got worse. Shortly after arriving, Pete's dad began to abuse his wife and children. He also began to abuse alcohol. Within months he had left the family. Pete described a difficult and confusing childhood and adolescence that ended with him dropping out of school and entering a life of delinquency. But the positive attitude and demeanor that I saw in the guy sitting two seats over was what allowed him to set out to change the course of his life when he hit his early twenties. He got his GED and started looking for a job. After landing a job with a national retail chain, he quickly worked his way up the ladder to the corporate office, where he was now employed as a district manager.

> I started to look around for the hidden cameras. I knew God wasn't answering my prayers for sleep, but the next two hours could be a pretty exciting answer to prayers.

Still, he was extremely unfulfilled. He felt his life had no purpose. He was consciously examining several faith systems, including Christianity. He had a girlfriend who wanted to get married but he couldn't bring himself to that point, nor could he make sense of his fear of commitment. His endless string of questions to me fell into a number of categories: Who is God? What is love? What is the purpose of my life?

Opie Doesn't Live Here Anymore

I was surprised that the two hours had gone by so fast when the plane finally touched down. Good conversation has a way of making that happen. Pete was an incredible guy. I could only hope that my words to him made sense as I had shared parts of my story in response to his questions. I didn't try to solve all his problems and I avoided all the tacky and empty Christian clichés I've heard (and sometimes used) over the years. I hoped that by telling Pete how God's story had shaped my story he might be challenged to reconsider his previous reservations about Christianity.

As we unfastened our seat belts and I popped in another breath mint, we exchanged business cards and promised to keep in touch. Pete quickly stood up and blew me away with what he said next: "I want to thank you for taking the time to listen to me. You're the best listener I've ever met." All that went through my mind was that Francis Schaeffer was right! That was the first time I'd ever been so accused by anybody.

Then Pete went on . . . and I'll take the liberty to use his exact words: "Thanks for not getting pissed off at me." "What?" I responded in a surprised manner. "Yeah, thanks for not getting pissed off at me. I've had lots of conversations with Christians and you're the first one that didn't get pissed off at me. Usually Christians get mad at me when I ask my honest questions or share my honest confusion about Christianity." I think I muttered a confused and emphatic "You're kidding me?" in response. Then, of course, I thought about the Christians I know and I realized what he was saying was true. I think I've been on the sending and receiving side in many of those same conversations.

Finally, as we started to make our way down the aisle and off the plane, Pete looked at me and said something I'll never forget: "This has been the most significant conversation I've ever had in my life." While I was grateful to God that I could be a part of it, it saddened me deeply to think that two hours talking to a tired and self-centered stranger could be more significant than any conversation he had shared in more than thirty years of life.

My heavenly Father smacked me upside the head with a few things that night. They're realities we need to hand on to the emerging generations of Christ's followers that we know, love, and have been called to minister to. Perhaps if we pound it into them now through our words and example, they won't make the same mistakes we've made, jump to some of our same stupid conclusions, or fall into any of our sad and sorry habits—behaviors that leave the world hoping and praying that they won't get stuck sitting in a seat next to us.

> ## My heavenly Father smacked me upside the head with a few things that night.

First, Christians can be real jerks. I stand at the front of the line. Thankfully, and by the grace of God, Pete hadn't seen my selfish heart that night. Oh, believe me, it was there. Thankfully—and by that same grace—God showed that same heart to me. Maybe it's time to stop writing off the world's seeming disdain for us to "the offensiveness of the cross." Perhaps those of us who represent Christ are so offensive that a needy and watching world never gets to the point where it even sees the cross.

Second, Pete reminded me how much I love spending time with people who have yet to experience God's transforming mercy and grace. It's too easy to be like the Pharisee who had Jesus over for dinner. When the sinful woman came by for a visit and wound up perfuming and kissing Jesus' feet, the Pharisee questioned Jesus' claims and credentials: "If this man were a prophet, he would know who is touching him and what kind of woman she is—that she is a sinner" (Luke 7:39). There's something wonderful, refreshing, and real about being with sinners like that. As his kingdom representatives, we better make sure we're taking his hands and his feet into their world.

Third, there's a world full of people desperate for connections. They're waiting for that "most significant" conversation. Some, like Pete, are so desperate that they're doing everything they can to make it happen. We won't be a part of what they're seeking if we're only praying for opportunities to be left alone so we can curl up in the corner by ourselves and fall asleep—or do whatever else it is we think is so important.

Fourth, listening is connecting. I didn't do a whole lot of talking. I didn't walk Pete through some pre-rehearsed presentation of the gospel that I learned back in my college days. But when I did open my mouth to talk about the faith, it was obvious that it was my open ears—and not my open mouth—that opened Pete's ears to hear the little I did have to say.

And finally, God never ceases to be full of surprises. I guess I shouldn't be surprised.

I made it to Dallas that night. But when my head finally hit the pillow, it was spinning so fast with excitement that I found it hard to sleep. It didn't matter. Everything that mattered had already happened, and I couldn't stop thinking about it.

WHOLLY, HOLY . . . OR HOLE-LY?

Youthculture@today; December 2003

Over the course of my forty-seven years on this earth, I've been called lots of names. Some are repeatable. Some are not. I've heard them on the playground, in the heat of competition, and from irate drivers who think I spend too much time in the left-hand lane. I've also been habitually referred to as "YOU IDIOT!" by none other than, well . . . me. I have a tendency to address myself this way when, among other things, I carelessly miscalculate a cut on the table saw, lose a computer file I forgot to save, or shank a backyard punt into the side of my neighbor's house. (When am I ever going to learn?!)

The old "sticks and stones" adage has always served me well, until recently anyway, when, in the midst of a discussion about the proper relationship between Christians and the world, someone more or less connected our approach to understanding and engaging the world of popular culture with promoting pornography. "So what you're saying is that Christians should know the culture?" I was asked. My excited answer was rather straightforward: "Yes, if God in his Word charges us to reach the world with the Good News about Jesus Christ, we must understand the changing cultural context in which lost people live. To do that, anyone who works with kids needs to be familiar with what they're watching and hearing—that's the stuff shaping their worldview. By doing that, we can learn how they think and what they believe. Then we'll be

able to connect with them in language and categories they can understand, and the unchanging, life-changing, and corrective truths of God's Word won't fall on deaf ears. In effect, we're cross-cultural missionaries!"

Case closed—or so I thought. The immediate response indicated otherwise: "So you tell those who want to reach kids to watch pornography?!?!?!" Wow! "Pornographer!"— that's one I never heard on the playground! OK, so the person didn't intend to lump me in with Hugh Hefner and Larry Flynt. Nor did he accuse me of producing pornography. But somehow, in his mind, I wasn't sharing the gospel anymore. Instead, I was promoting pornography and leading people down the compromising road to perdition. Ouch. Those sticks and stones really hurt.

> **Pornography is an expression of sinful and fallen sexuality and it certainly isn't a place where God wants us to go.**

To be honest, I've heard variations on this argument dozens of times before, so it really wasn't anything new. I responded as I have for years. First, I clarified that pornography is an expression of sinful and fallen sexuality and it certainly isn't a place where God wants us to go. Nor is it a place I indirectly suggest people go. It's not a legitimate art form that in and of itself is redeemable. We know that it's left a trail of destroyed individuals, marriages, and families in its ugly wake. It's to be avoided.

Neither would I suggest to a parent or youth worker that they go look at pornography if they discover their kids are spending time in it themselves. If I discovered my son was spending his time in some of the deepest and darkest corners of the Internet, I wouldn't say, "Hey buddy, let's sit down and look at this together so we can talk about it." That would be not only wrong, but ridiculous. I've seen it. He's seen it. Neither of us needs to see it again. But because I've seen it and know where it comes from, what it is, and what it does, I would sit down with him and talk about it.

> I wouldn't say, "Hey buddy, let's sit down and look at this together so we can talk about it." I've seen it. He's seen it. Neither of us needs to see it again.

Second, I challenged the faulty logic followed in the argument. My inquisitor had fallen into the classic mistake of employing the flawed "slippery slope" approach to logic. In his mind, if A happens (in this case, embracing the belief that "anyone who works with kids and wants to effectively share the gospel should be familiar with what they see and hear"), then through a series of small steps through B, C, D, and so on, eventually X, Y, and Z will happen—and Z is "You're promoting pornography!" Then, because Z shouldn't happen, A shouldn't happen either. If that's the case, then Jesus, Paul, and every cross-cultural missionary since has messed up big-time.

The conversation continued and it became abundantly clear to me that the root issue wasn't necessarily pornography. Rather, it was our differing understandings of what it means to be holy. We both agreed that God calls us to be holy. But we parted ways on how we are to live and conduct ourselves in our sinful and fallen world. In my friend's understanding, to be holy meant he was required to avoid contact of any type with the ungodly

Opie Doesn't Live Here Anymore

elements of popular culture. In my understanding, we've been commanded to go into that culture.

Because of the question I had been asked and the conclusions that had been reached, I decided I should regroup and humbly reevaluate my understanding of *holiness*. What if I've been wrong all this time? After all, I don't want to defend, promote, live, or teach a flawed understanding that isn't faithful to God's will for those who are his own. In order to check the validity of my understanding of how to approach matters of faith and culture, I needed to take another look at my understanding of holiness.

> Because of the question I had been asked and the conclusions that had been reached, I decided I should regroup and humbly reevaluate my understanding of holiness. What if I've been wrong all this time?

My trip back to square one had to start with the only truly holy one. What does he say in his Word about holiness? And rather than make the mistake of looking at and interpreting a few isolated verses on the subject, I needed to examine the full context of Scripture— examining all the parts of the Bible from start to finish as a comprehensive worldview. What did I find? Stated simply, here's a short summary of what the Bible says about holiness.

Holiness is first and foremost a divine quality. In fact, the word captures the essential nature of God and includes all his other attributes of sovereignty, mercy, awesomeness, separateness, power, wrath, and more. When the Bible speaks of God's holiness, it means that God and only God is morally perfect, and God and only God is uniquely set apart from all his creation. No one who has walked this earth—besides the God-man, Jesus—has ever, by nature, been holy. It's a truth we sing every time these words cross our lips: *Only Thou art holy; there is none beside Thee / Perfect in power, in love and purity.*[5]

> **This is the service for which we've been set apart! To do otherwise is to keep the Christian faith locked up behind a high wall of separation and fear.**

To be holy is to be set apart by God. We are declared and become holy the moment God, by grace, brings us into a relationship with himself through Christ. The source of our holiness is Jesus himself, who makes us holy by forgiving our sins. There's absolutely nothing we can do to make ourselves or anyone else holy. Our holiness, righteousness, and redemption are in Christ. As the writer of Hebrews put it, "We have been made holy through the sacrifice of the body of Jesus Christ" (Hebrews 10:10).

To be holy is to be consecrated for service to God. We are called to be set apart to serve our creator. As a result, we are to distance ourselves from the ways and values of the world. Even though we are holy in the eyes of God, we continue to struggle with sin—something I know the reality of all too well. We must prayerfully seek to separate ourselves from sin and hold fast to Christ. To be holy means to be different.

Jesus is not only the source of but also the standard and example of holiness. Holiness is the opposite of sinfulness. That means it represents conformity to the character of

Opie Doesn't Live Here Anymore

God and obedience to his will. We are to actively seek to express our new life in Christ and our holiness by following the example of Jesus. To be holy means that we will prayerfully and earnestly strive to avoid sin while reflecting his image in how we love others both inside and outside the body of Christ. "Holy, holy, holy" is the short answer to the great question Dean Borgman insists we ask as we minister in our contemporary culture: "How would Jesus move through the crowd today?"[6]

Holy people live the will of God, including his call to be "in" but "not of" the world. This is the great paradox of holiness—that the God who calls us to be "set apart" turns around and tells us to go into the sinful and fallen world, both through the example of his Son and the commands of Scripture. On the night before his death, Jesus prayed the will of his Father for all his disciples, in all times and in all places: "My prayer is not that you take them out of the world but that you protect them from the evil one. They are not of the world, even as I am not of it. . . . As you sent me into the world, I have sent them into the world" (John 17:15, 16, 18).

Looking at, listening to, and understanding that world for the sake of the advancement of God's rule and reign is not a compromise of our holiness. Instead, it's an expression of it. It's clearly part of the role God's called us to play in his grand plan of redemption. This is the service for which we've been set apart! To do otherwise is to keep the Christian faith locked up behind a high wall of separation and fear.

To be holy doesn't mean we keep a long list of behavioral dos and don'ts. Sadly, this is the un-biblical reality many have adopted simply because that's what they were taught growing up. This was exactly the problem with the Pharisees; they mistakenly believed that it was what's outside a person, rather than what's inside, that made him unclean. Charles Colson warns us of four problems bred by this view of holiness: First, it limits the scope of true biblical holiness to just a few, but not all, areas of our lives. We wind up living "out of" and not "in" the world, thereby forfeiting our mission influence. Second, we fall into the trap of obeying rules rather than obeying God. Third, the emphasis on rule-keeping leads us to believe we can be holy through our efforts. And fourth, our "pious efforts" can lead to self-righteousness—an ego-gratifying spirituality that turns holy living into spiritual one-upmanship.[7] The apostle Paul once lived that pharisaical life. But after experiencing God's grace on the road to Damascus and coming to a proper understanding of holiness, he referred to that old way of living as "dung" (Philippians 3:8, *The Message*).

> **We can't go places that we can't go. Christ has never called us to deliberately sin in order to engage the world for the sake of the gospel.**

Finally, we can't go places that we can't go. Christ has never called us to deliberately sin in order to engage the world for the sake of the gospel. If you can't watch it, listen to it, or read it without falling into sin, then don't.

But don't fall into the trap of equating temptation with sin. We know that Jesus, our example of holiness, was tempted in every way—but did not sin. Being tempted or even plagued by evil thoughts isn't sin. If a lustful or ungodly thought enters our mind and we choose to

Opie Doesn't Live Here Anymore

reject it, we have not sinned. But if we seek, embrace, or entertain those thoughts for the purpose of pursuing their pleasures, we've fallen into sin. Martin Luther likened the tension to the fact that evil thoughts will come like the birds that fly over our heads. That happens all the time; that's out of our control. What we can and must do is stop them from building nests in our hair. And lest we forget, the one who was tempted in every way but did not sin promises us that we won't be tempted beyond what we can bear, nor will he leave us without a way out (Hebrews 4:15, 1 Corinthians 10:13)! Maybe our problem is that we wind up trying to do God's work—imparting holiness—because we don't take him at his word.

> **Don't fall into the trap of equating temptation with sin. We know that Jesus, our example of holiness, was tempted in every way—but did not sin.**

I love how John Stott sums up the implications of the biblical view of holiness. He says "that the whole church is called—and every member of it—as much to involvement in the world as to separation from it, as much to 'worldliness' as to 'holiness.' Not to a worldliness which is unholy, nor to a holiness which is unworldly, but to 'holy worldliness,' a true separation to God which is lived out in the world—the world which he made and sent his Son to redeem."[8]

As our battle with the world, the flesh, and the devil rages on, we've got to be holy. There's no doubt about that. But our definition of holiness will determine whether we're in or out of the battle, on or off the battlefield. When my son's senior season of high school football came to an end back in November, I got to thinking about how much his weekly preparations for game time reflect how God's holy people are called to relate to the world. Every Saturday morning, while the bumps and bruises were still throbbing, Josh and his teammates would gather and watch the film of the previous night's game. They would evaluate how they played while looking to build on their strengths and correct their mistakes. Then, before they would take the practice field at the start of the following week, they would gather in the same film room to watch the tape of their opponent's last game. Even before they started their physical preparations for the next Friday night, they were working to know more about their opponent than that team knew about itself. When game time finally arrived, they would put everything they had learned and practiced into action, all in an effort to win.

But the analogy does break down. Yes, we've been called to battle. But it's not the lights on the scoreboard and what they show when the clock hits 00:00 that's at stake. Rather, it's about people who are lost and wandering aimlessly in the dark. Consequently, we need to be prepared.

Julia Ward Howe wrote the lyrics to "The Battle Hymn of the Republic" during the Civil War. While Abraham Lincoln's love for the song has led to its long association with the war, it actually was written as a testimony to the enduring nature of God's purpose, plan, and truth. As I've revisited what it means to be holy, I've realized that one of the song's last and most familiar lines encapsulates the truth about the source of our holiness and our response to it: *As he died to make men holy, let us die to make men free.*

For all those who come to the end of a life lived boldly with that understanding, there's going to be some name-calling. By the grace of God, I trust that all of us who have lived a theology of faith and culture that is "wholly holy"— and not one full of holes—will stand before the master as he says, "Well done, good and faithful servant."

WATCH WHAT YOU PRAY FOR

Youthculture@today; September 2005

Dave made me sick. He made me so sick that I've been unable to forget his rude, selfish, and obnoxious remarks— twenty-four years after he said them. It was Labor Day 1981 and I was with Dave and four other teenagers from my youth group boating in the clear blue waters of the Atlantic off the coast of Miami. We were enjoying the beautiful weather while swimming and water-skiing off the back end of a pretty impressive boat that belonged to Dave's father. When it was Dave's turn to ski, I went to the back of the boat to slide him the skis while he dove into the water. When he came up out of the water, he leaned back and let out a comfortable, mocking, and self-righteous sigh. "Ahhhh," he said. "I wonder what the poor people are doing today?" I couldn't believe it.

My disgust with Dave didn't last very long as my mind began processing his statement and the attitude that was its source. I quickly realized that his horrible words had probably captured the essence of how I was living my own life. If I was going to be mad, I was going to have to be mad at myself. If I was going to be sickened, it was because of the realization that Dave had verbalized not my own consciously held belief system (after all, I believe in Christ-like compassion), but my own everyday-embodied worldview. How could I effectively challenge Dave to love the poor when the man in my mirror was more or less living Dave's sickening statement?

In the years since that eye-opening moment, I've continued to think a lot about selfishness and self-centeredness and how they continue to manifest themselves in my life, our culture, the church, and our kids. When it comes to money and possessions, we've had so much for so long that we don't even realize how much we really have. But as actor Brad Pitt recently told Diane Sawyer as she was interviewing him about his relief efforts in Africa, if we are blessed to be born in America, we've "hit the lottery" and there's great responsibility that goes along with that.

> **Maybe we shouldn't be surprised if we see a selfish reflection of ourselves in the mirror of today's youth culture.**

Sadly, we followers of Jesus who should be leading the cultural charge against self-centered materialism are prone to follow the lead of the culture, rather than Christ, on this matter. When it comes to integrating our Christian faith into the material and financial parts of our lives, we're having difficulty. Kenneth Kantzer has said that "the most serious problem facing the church today is materialism—materialism not as a philosophical theory, but as a way of life."[9] I would agree. Materialism is the least recognized and most unaddressed sin of the American church and its members—of which I am one. Perhaps Dave and the following generations of Christian teens have learned well from myself and other adults who, as Tom Sine says, "all seem to be trying to live the American Dream with a little Jesus overlay. We talk about the lordship of Jesus, but our career comes first. Our house in the 'burbs comes first. Then, with whatever we have left, we try to follow Jesus."[10] Maybe we shouldn't be surprised if we see a selfish reflection of ourselves in the mirror of today's youth culture.

Five years ago, the volume on these issues was turned up in my head once again by the release and immediate popularity of Bruce Wilkinson's little ninety-two-page book, *The Prayer of Jabez: Breaking Through to the Blessed Life*. No doubt, most of you are probably already very familiar with this bestseller that expounds on two verses (1 Chronicles 4:9, 10) found in the middle of nine full chapters of genealogies contained in 1 Chronicles. If you haven't heard of it, you've either been asleep or you've failed to interact with one of the millions of Christians whose fervor for Jabez and his prayer has led them to lay out millions of dollars to purchase the various versions of *The Prayer of Jabez* and other Jabez memorabilia and, yes, even kitsch sold in bookstores—Christian and otherwise. Almost immediately, many of my more thoughtful and biblically literate friends humbly expressed disbelief at how quickly "Jabez fever" was sweeping through the church as, everywhere you turned, someone else was telling you with Amway-like enthusiasm about how they were embracing the prayer ("and you should too!"), praying it daily ("and you should too!"), and expecting God to release great blessings into their life ("and you should too!"). Christians who had never before read a book on prayer were devouring *The Prayer of Jabez*.

I wasn't surprised at all. While I'm guessing Wilkinson's intent was otherwise, and I'm sure not everyone who embraced the prayer prayed it in this way, it seemed that asking the Lord to "bless me and enlarge my territory!"

and to "let your hand be with me, and keep me from harm so that I will be free from pain" was a new and popular way for many to ask God for more stuff and an easier life. Could it be that an obscure Old Testament passage was being marketed (yes, marketed! . . . and effectively!) to a twenty-first century American church that was eager to find biblical justification to have more? Perhaps the Jabez phenomenon and its rapid embrace as a mechanized and magical mantra is the greatest indicator of how self-centered and materialistic we've become. It plays well in our wealthy, market-driven, consumer-oriented, narcissistic, North American Christian culture. In many ways the prayer of Jabez has become a formulaic and convenient prayer that we've lifted out of its biblical context (author Gary Gilley recognizes this in his book *"I Just Wanted More Land"—Jabez*[11]) and twisted to cater to our skewed values in order to further our desires, redeem our materialism, and justify our greed. And all this is done without even knowing that's what we've done. After all, praying more earnestly and regularly is a good thing, isn't it?

> Perhaps the Jabez phenomenon and its rapid embrace as a mechanized and magical mantra is the greatest indicator of how self-centered and materialistic we've become.

Let me admit that if I had prayed the prayer of Jabez myself, I would be prone to ask God to do "my will" rather than "thy will." I see and know the ugly reality of my heart. For that reason, I couldn't pray the prayer. Yes, I ask God for blessing and protection every day. But while I oftentimes catch myself wanting more stuff, the fact is that I already have far more material "territory" than

Opie Doesn't Live Here Anymore

I need. Somehow, stating these reasons to many of my Jabez-loving friends made me less spiritual in their eyes.

> Let me admit that if I had prayed the prayer of Jabez myself, I would be prone to ask God to do "my will" rather than "thy will."

But the wonderful reality of life—both in Bible times and today—is that God often blesses us most deeply when the very things that we erroneously equate with his blessings are withheld, thereby gifting us with an opportunity to experience the blessing of living our lives under his reign and rule with complete dependence on him. Oh, we may say we live that way already. But why, then, do third-world Christians who scrape for food, clothing, and shelter while living in material poverty have a fervor, joy, selfless depth, and richness to their faith that puts us—and I include myself here in this critique—to shame? And this is while we walk around prone to dissatisfaction with what we already have, desiring more, and consumed with wanting to live a life free from God's gift of pain?

The sad result of our prosperity and desire for even more is that we've become even more prosperous and desiring of even more. All the while, we fool ourselves into believing that we are entitled to it all and that we are walking the path of discipleship. This is why more is said in the New Testament about money and wealth than about Heaven and Hell combined. This is why five times more is said about money than about prayer. This is why sixteen of Christ's thirty-eight parables deal with money. This is why Jesus said, "Do not store up for yourselves treasures on earth, where moth and rust destroy, and where thieves break in and steal. But store up for yourselves treasures in heaven, where moth and rust do not destroy, and where thieves do not break in and steal. For where your treasure is, there your heart will be also" (Matthew 6:19-21).

> The sad result of our prosperity and desire for even more is that we've become even more prosperous and desiring of even more.

It's because of the dangerous and consuming grip this reality gets on us that Jesus said, "It is easier for a camel to go through the eye of a needle than for a rich man to enter the kingdom of God" (Matthew 19:24). This is why the apostle Paul warned, "People who want to get rich fall into temptation and a trap and into many foolish and harmful desires that plunge men into ruin and destruction. For the love of money is the root of all kinds of evil. Some people, eager for money, have wandered from the faith and pierced themselves with many griefs" (1 Timothy 6:9, 10). And this is why Ron Sider, in his book *The Scandal of the Evangelical Conscience*, writes, "The gospel of individual self-fulfillment now reigns" and "by their daily behavior, most Christians regularly commit treason. With their mouths they claim that Jesus is Lord, but with their actions they demonstrate allegiance to money, sex, and self-fulfillment."[12]

Sadly, our current generation of children and teens are choosing to follow in our self-centered and materialistic footsteps. Contrary to the opinion of some, the emerging generations haven't turned their backs on the materialism of their parents. Instead, they're embracing it. I remember

Opie Doesn't Live Here Anymore

how optimistic many of the culture-watchers were back at the end of the '80s. They believed that the end of the "me decade" and Reaganomics would be accompanied by a parallel demise of greed and materialism among children and teens. In the '90s, generational researchers picked up on this trend, predicting that the millennial generation would forsake materialism for social activism. While I wish I could have been anything but skeptical about those predictions, skepticism—or more accurately "realism"—was in order. Young hearts that long to be filled by God continue to embrace money and the things money buys, believing that "more" leads to more joy and more fulfillment. Nothing could be further from the truth. Unfortunately, young and old hearts that profess to be filled by God continue to embrace the same lies, often reducing the infinite and awesome God of the universe to a personal genie who takes our wishes and turns them into his commands.

> Contrary to the opinion of some, the emerging generations haven't turned their backs on the materialism of their parents. Instead, they're embracing it.

A few months ago I saw the fruit of our culture's systemic materialism when I attended the "Kid Power 2005" marketing conference. Three hundred and fifty marketers—along with one curious outsider who did nothing but listen—spent a few intense days sharing secrets on how to market to kids. Their definition of "kids"? Two- to twelve-year-olds! I watched and listened in amazement as presenters talked about how to "reach," "preach to," "build relationships with," and "evangelize" the most targeted market segment in the world. Why? Because those kids have, spend, and influence the spending of more money than any other age group. In effect, the conference was all about creating and cultivating lifelong consumers who will grow up constantly seeking to meet a growing list of market-formulated and reformulated "needs" in an effort to finally be made whole. Our distorted adaptation of Jabez's prayer plays well in that kind of world.

> Something about our unique times, today's youth culture, and my own situation made the prayer of a man named Agur jump out at me like never before.

You might now be wondering what's occasioned my somewhat harsh rants and ramblings about kids, materialism, and what we've done with the prayer of Jabez. At one level, it's the reality of what I see when I look at today's youth culture. At another level, it's the reality of the example I see when I examine my own life. It's also our failure to understand and live the kingdom of God as lived and taught by our Savior. And it's the fact that earlier this year I stumbled upon another Old Testament prayer that seems to be timely and worth embracing. Try as hard as I can, I can't get that prayer out of my head, most likely because it needs to be the prayer of my heart.

I'm sure I've run across it numerous times before in my readings of Proverbs 30. But something about our unique times, today's youth culture, and my own situation made the prayer of a man named Agur jump out at me like never before. Agur prays, "Two things I ask of you, O Lord; do not refuse me before I die: Keep falsehood and lies far from me; give me neither poverty nor riches, but give me only my daily bread. Otherwise, I may have too much and disown you and say, 'Who is the Lord?' Or I may become poor and steal, and so dishonor the name of my God" (Proverbs 30:7-9).

> **When I compare myself to Donald Trump, I can easily rationalize away any materialism and see myself as "poor."**

All Agur begged for was to speak the truth, and to have just what was necessary for him to remain committed and obedient to his God. Jesus taught his disciples to pray for the same. Agur understood human nature and he knew his weakness. In wisdom, he prayed to be rich in faithfulness. I'm not sure Agur's prayer would sell—as books, trinkets, and kitsch—in today's Christian market. That's too bad. It's a challenging prayer that shakes up our prevailing attitudes and reflects God's will, way, and kingdom priorities. It's a God-centered prayer that focuses on "thy will" and not "my will," as we ask God to bless by giving and withholding as he pleases.

When I compare myself to Donald Trump, I can easily rationalize away any materialism and see myself as "poor." But if I were to stand with the world's population in a line starting with the richest and ending with the poorest, I would be—along with you, my kids, and perhaps the entire North American church—in the front 5 percent of the line. So, the prayer of Agur is looking pretty necessary.

We'd do well to heed the warning C.S. Lewis issues in *The Screwtape Letters*. He writes, "Prosperity knits a man to the world. He feels that he is finding his place in it, while really it is finding its place in him."[13]

I guess the real question we should all be asking of ourselves, our church, and our kids is this: "Ahhhh . . . I wonder what the rich people are doing today?" Watch what you pray for.

Raise Your Hand!

Youthculture@today; March 2006

OK . . . this one might get me in some trouble. And it's all because I'm increasingly convinced that we're doing something wrong in youth ministry. We've been chugging along thinking we've been doing it right. As a result, we continue to do it wrong because we think it's right, and in doing so, we're undermining the very work of the very God we pride ourselves in serving. Confused yet? Let me explain.

What's prompted my thinking on this matter is a publicity piece I recently read regarding a self-described youth evangelist who touts his "success" by advertising the fact that he's led more than one million kids to Christ. Sorry, I just can't take that too seriously. I wish I could, but I can't. To be fair, this isn't the first time I've heard claims like this.

My hesitancy to trust the numbers started way back in the late 1970s when, as a college student, I attended a conference where evangelist Tom Skinner was the keynote speaker. I can still visualize Skinner, a brilliant man whose passion was deep, talking about the waning influence of the church on American culture. In an effort to challenge us to take our faith seriously, Skinner asked a thought-provoking question that has stuck with me since: "George Gallup's research tells us that fifty million Americans describe themselves as 'born-again Christians,'" Skinner said. This was great news—until Skinner lowered the boom that rocked my simple and satisfying world. He soberly asked: "If there are fifty million born-again Christians in America, where are they?" Skinner's question, and the reality it exposed, has haunted me for twenty-five years. I thought about it again when I read the youth evangelist's claim.

> Rarely do we go back a year later to see if the raised hand yielded a radically changed life. If we did, our math would have to include a little less addition and a lot more subtraction.

I'm guessing the "successful" youth evangelist has probably (or maybe) seen more than a million kids walk forward or raise their hands in response to his invitation to "make a decision" for Christ. I'm in no position to judge his motives or the accuracy of his numbers. But I think we can, and should, question his—and our—quality control. Part of the problem lies in the very fact that we spend so much time counting up the numbers so that we can judge our success, validate the effectiveness of our ministries, and look good when we report back to our supervisors and church boards. Rarely do we go back a year later to see if the raised hand yielded a radically changed life. If we did, our math would have to include a little less addition and a lot more subtraction.

The reason? We're so focused on getting kids' hands up that we don't offer a way for the one who raised the hand to learn about the necessity and shape of the changed life that should begin the minute the hand goes down. Or, even more troubling, we focus only on getting kids' hands up because our theology of salvation has failed to include a place for what happens afterward.

The result? Add up the numbers that are yours, mine, and everybody else's. Pretty impressive, huh? Until we ask the same question Skinner asked more than a quarter-century ago: "Where are they?"

> **Do kids know that there's a life of integrating faith into every minute and every activity that's to be lived between the second their hand goes up and the second their heart stops beating?**

That question should force us to ask ourselves some other questions. As parents and youth workers, we invite the kids we know and love to commit their lives to Christ— and we should! But are we taking the time to explain what a life of following Christ here on this earth is all about, how difficult it is, and what it requires? Do we ever talk about the fact that following the God-man who bled and suffocated on the cross requires his followers to take up a cross of their own? Do kids know that there's a life of integrating faith into every minute and every activity that's to be lived between the second their hand goes up and the second their heart stops beating? In order to come away with affirmative answers to each of these questions, we might have to rethink our understanding of conversion— that wrong thing that we've been thinking we've had right for so long. Perhaps if we understood conversion, then our ministries, our kids, our understanding of success, our numbers, and most importantly our world, would look markedly different.

For too long, youth ministry has been about getting kids "saved." I struggle with our definition of what it means to be saved and the methods we employ to get young people saved. In his thought-provoking book on conversion, *Beginning Well*, Gordon Smith says that the church is guilty of thinking of conversion in "minimalist terms: What is the very least that a person needs to do in order to be freed from the horrors of Hell and assured of the glories of Heaven?"[14] Dallas Willard calls this the "gospel of sin management," that belief that forgiveness alone is what Christianity is all about.[15] It's a faith that has nothing else to do with the rest of your life. You've raised your hand, you've walked forward, and now you're saved. And while it's probably not intentional, we then proceed to leave the impression that all there is to do now is get on with life . . . until the next time you hear the invitation and say yes again—kind of like adding another rider onto your eternal life insurance policy.

> For some, conversion is only about exchanging your one-way tickct to Hell for a guaranteed ticket to Heaven— a ticket you cash in when life on this earth ends.

For some, conversion is only about exchanging your one-way ticket to Hell for a guaranteed ticket to Heaven—a ticket you cash in when life on this earth ends. Until then, you continue to live your life as you choose. Conversion has nothing to do with this life except living with the assurance of Heaven in the next. The result is that there's nothing that requires your life on earth to be marked by anything that sets you apart from others whose hands have never gone up.

For others, conversion is about a change in destination when life on this earth ends—from going to Hell to going to Heaven—and then making every opportunity while you're still here to tell other people how to do the same. While along with your conversion comes a new responsibility to witness in a way that gets more hands up in the air, life on this earth is really about separating yourself out of this world to keep yourself from getting poisoned by this world, while focusing your hopeful gaze on Heaven in anticipation of the day when your escape will be complete.

For both, the gospel is not so much about how you live your life now, but about where you'll live your afterlife then. In other words, it's entirely possible that there are fifty million self-described born-again Americans, and we have no clue where they are—either because they blend in, or they've run away to hide. The real problem with the "saved" is that they don't understand salvation.

It's time to understand and act on the fact that conversion is not just about belief, repentance, forgiveness, and eternal life. Something else has to happen after someone accepts Christ as Savior. Salvation makes us free from sin and slaves to righteousness. We are rebirthed people living every second of our new lives on this earth under the reign of the king who has made us his own by calling us into his kingdom. We are called onto the joyful path of integrating the Christian faith and the kingdom of God into all of life.

When we call young people to faith, we're not calling them out of the world and into Heaven. Instead, we're calling them to live God's will and God's way in the world. Believe it or not, Jesus didn't come just to save us from

Opie Doesn't Live Here Anymore

our sins. The way many of us have been raised makes this statement sound like heresy. But it's not. The real heresy is the belief that Jesus only came to save us from our sins. Think about this: when we pray the words *Your kingdom come, your will be done, on earth as it is in Heaven*, we are asking God to unleash his kingdom through us as we live his will and his way in every nook and cranny of our lives and his world. True conversion reorders and transforms both the now and then.

> When we call young people to faith, we're not calling them out of the world and into Heaven. Instead, we're calling them to live God's will and God's way in the world.

My hope and prayer is that my story will be swallowed up by God's story. My prayer for my kids is the same. If that's what happens when the hands go down, nobody will be left wondering where they are right now. And that's what it really means to say, "Yes, I want to be saved."

If that's the message we communicate in our youth ministries, when the kids' hands go down, those hands will be getting right to work. And for the rest of their earthly lives, it will be impossible for the world to miss seeing where they are.

THE CHURCH AND *THE PASSION*

Blog; February 17, 2004

Did you happen to catch Mel Gibson's interview with Diane Sawyer last night? I did, and the reason I watched is that I'm excited, like so many others, about the upcoming release of his highly publicized film,

The Passion of the Christ. Like you, I'm wondering how God will use the film to expand his kingdom. I'm praying that will certainly happen. But as I watched Gibson's interview, it suddenly dawned on me that God might just be using this film to challenge the church more than he will use it to challenge the world . . . and I'm not necessarily talking about deepening our understanding of the sacrifice Christ made on our behalf. Granted, that will happen and I hope it does. But there are four other significant issues this film and our attraction to it raise—and I hope we're listening and willing to learn.

First, evangelical Christians are excited about something made by a—hush!—conservative Catholic! I can't tell you how many times I've been hammered by fellow evangelicals for believing "Yes, a Catholic can be a justified and sanctified follower and lover of Jesus Christ." But now Gibson's become a darling of the evangelical community. And many who question the faith of Catholics—because those questioners are embracing his movie—are eating crow. Perhaps Gibson's *Passion*, and passion, will make us rethink such ridiculous conclusions. Granted, we won't see eye-to-eye with Gibson on every area of his theology. But the kingdom is certainly a lot bigger than some of us think.

Second, Christians who deny Gibson's faith and who don't go to movies (or listen to music, or watch TV, or read books, or . . .) that aren't made by Christians are in a real pickle. For the sake of consistency, you'd better not darken the door of a theater screening *The Passion*. But if you do—and I hope you will—you're recognizing (even though I think your conclusions on Gibson's faith are faulty) that God does indeed work his will and his ways

Opie Doesn't Live Here Anymore

through those who are not redeemed. Theologians call it "general revelation" and "common grace." Be careful—if you're a separatist who goes to the film and God uses it to speak to you and touch your life, you'll be letting God out of that nice little box you've had him in for so long. But that will be a good thing since he doesn't belong in there in the first place. And when you let him out of your box, you'll realize that he's been speaking LOUDLY through music, film, books, TV, and more ways that aren't "Christian," for a long, long time—and you've been missing out on a lot!

Third—and this is a biggie—the movie is rated R! I continue to be amazed and discouraged by the number of fellow believers who somehow think that not going to R-rated movies is a sign and guarantee of personal holiness. I don't buy that for a minute. First, are we crazy enough to trust the ratings as the dictate for what films we do and do not view? Second, do we realize that violence, sex, and profanity in film can be presented in a manner that is good, true, and right? Not all violence, sex, and profanity is gratuitous. I want and need to see the reality of the violence Christ suffered on my behalf. I want my kids to see the same. And third, do we realize that while an R-rated film could lead us into a deeper understanding of God and relationship with him, a G-rated film could present and portray a worldview that is totally contradictory to God's order and design for the world? If we pride ourselves on not going to R-rated movies, we'd better think twice before going to *The Passion*. Either we'll have to admit our standards have been narrow and our understanding of holiness skewed, or we'll have to stay home and stay "consistent."

And finally, did you catch Sawyer's report on the results of the poll on religion in America? I guess we should be happy that 82 percent of Americans are "Christians." Theologian David Wells says that if we believe numbers like these, we "have been living in a fool's paradise." He continues:

> When Gallup produced his figures in the 1970s, and has repeated them every year ever since, it seemed like evangelicals were on a roll with such wide popular support and with churches that were growing. It looked as though we were on the verge of sweeping all of our religious and cultural opponents before us. That was why these figures stirred such alarm in the secular media, why they created some heartburn in the mainline Protestant denominations, and why they produced just a little power-mongering amongst evangelicals. But it has turned out to be an optical illusion. The reality that we have to face today is that we have produced a plague of nominal evangelicalism which is as trite and as superficial as anything we have seen in Catholic Europe.[16]

If we're honest with ourselves, that 82 percent figure is embarrassing. Where are we? If "Christian" is only a label and not a lifestyle, the figure isn't surprising and we shouldn't be celebrating.

The same Jesus whose death Gibson's film portrays prayed the will of his Father the night before his death. That will? For his followers in all times and all places to be "in" but "not of" the world. Living that way requires we rethink our attitudes toward Catholic believers, where and how God chooses to work in the world, the stuff we do and don't watch, and how we integrate our faith into all of life.

Opie Doesn't Live Here Anymore

EMBRACING THE COLLISION

I hate, I despise your religious feasts; I cannot stand your assemblies. Even though you bring me burnt offerings and grain offerings, I will not accept them. Though you bring choice fellowship offerings, I will have no regard for them. Away with the noise of your songs! I will not listen to the music of your harps. But let justice roll on like a river, righteousness like a never-failing stream! (Amos 5:21-24)

Enter through the narrow gate. For wide is the gate and broad is the road that leads to destruction, and many enter through it. But small is the gate and narrow the road that leads to life, and only a few find it. (Matthew 7:13, 14)

Therefore, I urge you, brothers, in view of God's mercy, to offer your bodies as living sacrifices, holy and pleasing to God—this is your spiritual act of worship. (Romans 12:1)

1. DO YOU AGREE THAT THE INFLUENCES OF MARKETING have affected/infected the church? If so, how so?

2. HOW IS LISTENING CONNECTING? Why is listening so important if we are going to reach people with the gospel?

3. WHAT IS MEANT BY "HOLY WORLDLINESS"? How has this section of the book challenged your understanding of holiness from a biblical perspective?

4. DO YOU AGREE THAT THE CHURCH IS GUILTY of thinking of conversion in minimalist terms? How should we think about conversion?

Opie Doesn't Live Here Anymore

IS GOD NEAR?

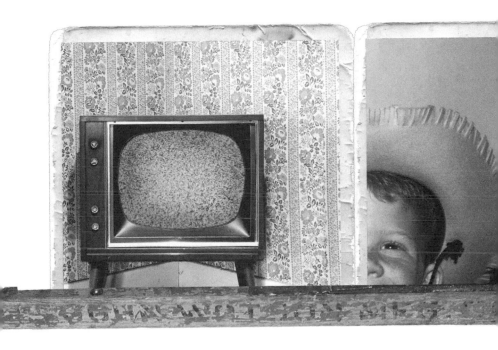

"GOD, ARE YOU OUT THERE?"

I've heard these words uttered in a variety of ways, shapes, and forms through the years by those who wonder if God is, indeed, out there. I've heard them at the movies, in music, on television, and from numerous flesh-and-blood acquaintances struggling to find their way through life devoid of a knowledge of, or relationship with, their creator.

"God, where are you?" I've heard these words uttered by those who already know God, but are left wondering and doubting if he's taken leave when they are locked in a battle with the sufferings of life. At times, these words have crossed my own lips. Feeling helpless, I've pleaded, along with the psalmist: "How long, O Lord? Will you forget me forever? How long will you hide your face from me?" (Psalm 13:1).

> God continues to reveal himself in his created order. He reveals himself in the image of himself that he stamped into every human being.

"Where is God?" There's an old saying that goes something like this: You can only be sure of two things in life—death and taxes. I've learned that the fact that God is, has been, and will always be is even more certain—*even when it doesn't feel that way*. From Genesis to Revelation, the Scriptures offer convincing evidence that this is true. The lives of the saints, those adopted as sons and daughters of God—both past and present—do the same.

God continues to reveal himself in his created order. He reveals himself in the image of himself that he stamped into every human being. He has made himself known through his Son, our Redeemer, Jesus Christ. And he lives in us in the person of the Holy Spirit. Perhaps the question shouldn't be "Is God near?" but "Why do we ever doubt his presence?"

God *is*. My thoughts in this section have been prompted by instances of seeing the obviousness of God where I might least expect him—and wondering where God might be when I most need him.

FRIDAY WAS GOOD!

Blog; January 30, 2006

If we're tuned in and really paying attention, the normal events of every day bring evidence of God's sovereignty, mercy, grace, and providence. People who have experienced the blessing of circumstances that force them to stop and take notice are typically the ones who remind the hurried rest of us of these things.

We've all heard stories of those who have experienced a traumatic life event—perhaps a sudden disability or loss of some function that the rest of us take for granted—who then go out of their way to remind us to "stop and smell the roses." My problem is that I let my normal life circumstances keep me so rushed and stressed that I miss the evidence of the greatness of God and his world in the "little things" that are much, much bigger than I typically recognize.

> My problem is that I let my normal life circumstances keep me so rushed and stressed that I miss the evidence of the greatness of God and his world in the "little things" that are much, much bigger than I typically recognize.

I'm deeply grateful to God that Friday wasn't one of those days. While it may be a bit odd for me to describe the day in reverse order, too bad. It all ended with Friday night. I decided one of those spur-of-the-moment activities was in order. I invited both of my boys to join me at a local venue known as The American Music Theatre. The place has been here in Lancaster for ten years and this was my first trip through its doors. Oh, I've seen their ads in our paper every week. But I've never really been drawn to a series of concerts that typically feature well-known musical has-beens that play to the older tourists who love coming to Lancaster for outlet shopping, all-you-can-eat buffets, and Amish sightings.

> **Calling it a tribute show makes it sound a bit cheesy—kind of like an Elvis show featuring a fat, old guy shoved into a tight and tacky polyester suit.**

Friday night was another story. The "Classical Mystery Tour" was in town. My nineteen-year-old son, Josh, home from college for the weekend, just lit up with energy when I suggested we go. The trip was on, and we grabbed thirteen-year-old Nate without telling him where we were headed . . . partly because he wouldn't have wanted to go if we had told him! After downing some tasty burgers, we headed down to get our tickets to the big show.

In case you haven't figured it out, the "Classical Mystery Tour" is one of those Beatles tribute shows. Calling it a tribute show makes it sound a bit cheesy—kind of like an Elvis show featuring a fat, old guy shoved into a tight and tacky polyester suit, wearing a pretty foul-looking wig, and trying as hard as he can to mimic the King. (And all this while a bunch of older women forget that they're older women and scream after him.) On this night, the difference existed in my mind because of my childhood and because my love for popular music was in many ways shaped by the Fab Four. In fact, the band spent about six years providing the soundtrack to my life, between the third and eighth grades. I remember exactly where I was and the deep shock and disappointment I felt when Steve King, a friend whose parents actually allowed him to grow his hair out like the Beatles (lucky kid!), showed up at the school bus stop and announced the news that the band had broken up. I saw "Beatlemania" back in the early '80s and it was pretty fascinating. About ten years ago I saw another Beatles show that was pretty good as well.

> Where was the greatness of God in it all? I saw it in humanity's ability to create, something the Beatles did so well as they lived out the image of God inherent in who they were as talented musicians, writers, and innovators.

So the lights go down, and the guys come out on stage . . . looking, sounding, acting, playing, and singing like the real Fab Four back in February 1964. Before the night was out, they had changed clothes, hair, and musical styles to reflect everything from "The Magical Mystery Tour" to "Let It Be." I'm still dumbfounded at how much these four looked like the Beatles, moved like the Beatles, and sang like the Beatles—all while playing their instruments like the Beatles. The George Harrison clone even got a well-deserved standing ovation for his ax work on "While My Guitar Gently Weeps." The whole show was so good that I just sat there for two hours with my jaw dropped as I kept my eyes glued to the stage. Every once in a while Josh and I would glance at each other and just start laughing out loud—it was that realistic and enjoyable. And Nate? Well, he acted bored. Of course, he spent the better part of Saturday morning doing his household chores while singing "I Want to Hold Your Hand" at the top of his lungs. When I asked him what he was doing, he told me the song was stuck in his head. Hmmmmm. Isn't that what the Beatles' music used to do to me when I was his age?

So where was the greatness of God in it all? I saw it in humanity's ability to create, something the Beatles did so well as they lived out the image of God inherent in who they were as talented musicians, writers, and innovators. I saw it in the enjoyment that the music brought to hundreds of other people sitting with us in that theater. I saw it in Josh's eyes, smile, laugh, and his "Thanks so much for taking me, Dad. That was great!" I saw it when I heard the John Lennon imposter do a dead-on rendition of "Imagine," a song that forced me to think about Lennon's utopian dream and the fact that even though Lennon missed it, God had taken care of business two thousand years ago. It was a good night.

> "Imagine" forced me to think about Lennon's utopian dream and the fact that even though Lennon missed it, God had taken care of business two thousand years ago.

It followed a good afternoon. One of the highlights— if I dare call it that—was something Josh and I witnessed that perhaps only someone from Lancaster County could really appreciate. We were driving back from visiting my dad, and we found ourselves following a short, yellow school bus. The bus was stopping every couple hundred yards or so to drop off Amish children at the end of their long farm lanes. At the last stop, a quartet of Amish siblings hopped off and started up their drive—two girls and two boys. A few steps into their journey up the lane, one of those sibling fights we "English" witness far too often in our homes broke out, with a younger brother going full bore into his older sister with his water bottle, boots, and fists. Her hope for escape—which, by the way, didn't work out, at least not while we were still looking over our shoulders while driving away—took her into one of the family's fields. Now, please don't think that I'm the kind of guy who takes pleasure in another's violence or misfortune, but something about what we were seeing really struck Josh and me as funny! Perhaps it was the fact that we had just been talking about his upcoming return to school, where he is going to start a theology class that looks at violence and nonviolence in the Bible. Because he attends an Anabaptist-related college, he's already aware of what perspective will be taught as the correct option. Considering the fact that this boy of mine still considers joining the Army infantry as a career option, I think he's going to be doing a lot of squirming in that class!

> He can't move much at all and his muscles
> are getting more and more atrophied.
> But through it all we visit, laugh, and talk.

But back to the Amish kids. I think what really got to us was the visual evidence that even though the Amish are known to be peaceful people, we saw firsthand that they are just as fallen and in need of both self-control and rescue from anger as the rest of us. And right there in that visual reminder of our need and the divine provision for that need was an awareness of the goodness and grace of our God.

> My dad lifted his head ever-so-slightly off his pillow and said, ever-so-faintly, "Psalm 46."

That all followed a good early afternoon. Josh and I had traveled up to the nursing care facility in which my dad's been living since his debilitating stroke. Dad's still struggling. He's learning to talk through his trach hole and he's doing much better, even though it's sometimes labored and very difficult to understand. He still can't swallow and he's eating through a feeding tube. He can't move much at all and his muscles are getting more and more atrophied. But through it all we visit, laugh, and talk. On Friday, he really enjoyed seeing Josh. My mom was there as well. Then, one of my pastors came by to visit Dad. Being a pastor himself who is so new to the area that he never got settled into a church, my dad doesn't have a pastor in the Lancaster area. It was great to have Pastor John come by, and we had a wonderful visit. Dad and John connected well. When the visit was nearly over, John told Dad he'd like to read him a psalm and pray with us. As John began leafing through his Bible, he asked Dad if there was a psalm he would like to have read. My dad nodded his head, then lifted it ever-so-slightly off his pillow and pursed his lips as he got ready to talk. He looked at John and said, ever-so-faintly, "Psalm 46."

And then John read these words:

God is our refuge and strength, an ever-present help in trouble. Therefore we will not fear, though the earth give way and the mountains fall into the heart of the sea, though its waters roar and foam and the mountains quake with their surging. There is a river whose streams make glad the city of God, the holy place where the Most High dwells. God is within her, she will not fall; God will help her at break of day. Nations are in uproar, kingdoms fall; he lifts his voice, the earth melts. The Lord Almighty is with us; the God of Jacob is our fortress. Come and see the works of the Lord, the desolations he has brought on the earth. He makes wars cease to the end of the earth; he breaks the bow and shatters the spear, he burns the shields with fire. 'Be still, and know that I am God; I will be exalted among the nations, I will be exalted in the earth.' The Lord Almighty is with us; the God of Jacob is our fortress.

Yes, Friday was a good day.

LESSONS FROM JOHNNY

Blog; February 21, 2005

I'm a late-night guy who grew up watching Johnny Carson. Something about the guy's sense of humor always resonated with me. Since his death a few weeks ago, numerous magazines have been running retrospective and tribute articles on the man who defined and shaped late-night television.

The latest edition of *Rolling Stone* features a reprint of one of Johnny's rare interviews, which originally ran in the magazine back in 1979. I gave it a read the other day and was struck by something Carson said and did back in the early days of *The Tonight Show*. The interviewer said to Carson, "You don't have rock 'n' roll on the show." Carson responded with a story:

I had a group on once—I can't remember their name (the Youngbloods), but they were really hot. They didn't like the platform or the riser or the lights; they were talking to my director—who had only been directing for twenty-some years. So I told them to pack up and get the hell out of the building. I went on the air that night and I said, 'We had booked the so-and-so group. They didn't like the lights, they didn't like the directing, so I told them to go home, blow their noses, and when they grew up they could come back and be on the show.' And the audience applauded, because they had had it with that kind of behavior. With rock stars who have not been able to handle fame and money thrown at them, they mistake the recognition for importance. They're demanding this, they're demanding that, because they've heard that's the way you do it. [1]

I've been around the block enough to know that the experience Johnny had isn't just limited to the world of Hollywood entertainment. Big heads and egos are everywhere these days. Where I run into them most often is in the ghetto we've created that might be called Christian Hollywood. We've got our celebrities and stars, and our adoration and worship of them can certainly swell heads and inflate egos. Some even strut around with their entourage and shred forests with their reams of contract riders demanding this, that, and every other ridiculous thing. I know because I've heard the comments of frustrated people who've booked some of these folks and wound up tending to minutiae rather than doing ministry. What in the world have we become?

Funny how the one whose name we've hijacked and used in the label "Christian" never fell into that trap. He came to humbly serve. I need to be constantly reminded of that fact. I was thinking about this as I read Carson's comments and then reflected back on the fifteen years of ministry we're celebrating with CPYU. I always remind our staff and myself that ministry is a privilege and responsibility. There's nothing—absolutely nothing—special about us or anything we do that should cause us to puff up and think more highly of ourselves than we ought.

> **Funny how the one whose name we've hijacked and used in the label "Christian" never fell into that trap. He came to humbly serve. I need to be constantly reminded of that fact.**

I like to phrase this undeniable truth with a constant reminder I tell myself all the time: "What it all boils down to is this—you're nothing but a butthead who's been redeemed by grace." Once a butthead, always a butthead. I hope I've lived out my understanding of that fact well over the last fifteen years. My wife and kids will probably tell you that if I could brag about anything, that would be it! As I think about Carson's experience with the Youngbloods, I wonder who I may have offended over the years by thinking too highly of myself. If I've done that to you, I'm sorry.

THANKS BE TO GOD . . . WE WERE SPARED!

Blog; August 23, 2006

Since word is rapidly spreading about yesterday's excitement here at CPYU, I thought I'd recount the events of the morning. This will serve as testimony to God's amazing grace, mercy, and miraculous love . . . as each of these is what I experienced in deep ways yesterday.

Here's what happened—keep in mind that all this took only a few seconds.

I arrived in the CPYU office about 7:10 AM to do some writing. I went into my office, which sits on the corner of a one-story, brick office building. I sat at my desk—a U-shaped unit positioned in the outside corner of the building—and was checking and answering e-mail. My cell phone rang and I stood up to take it out of my pocket. While standing, I looked down at the phone and saw that my son Josh was calling. He was getting off a plane at Dulles and calling me with his connecting info. I said, "Hey, Josh." He answered, "Hey, Dad." While he was answering, I heard banging and skidding sounds outside the office. I glanced to the front window that views the two-lane main road in front of the office and saw some vehicles slowing down to stop. I said to Josh, "Hold on a minute." I leaned on my desk to look out the window and to the right to see if there had been an accident.

I remember thinking *The big bang is coming any second now*. Little did I realize how accurate that thought would be.

Immediately, I found myself looking straight into the wide eyes of a man who was looking straight in my direction as he gripped his steering wheel with both hands. He was about twenty feet from my window and traveling directly at me at about forty-five miles per hour. I instinctively jumped back and to the right and stood straight up with my feet together. Just as I did that, the car came right through the brick wall, stopping with the man where my desk had been. The best way for you to picture how it ended is this: it was as if he had skidded to a stop at a drive-through window, and I was peering down at him through his car window as he waited for me to hand him his order. The sound of wood splintering, bricks flying, and glass breaking was one I will never forget.

> Immediately, I found myself looking straight into the wide eyes of a man who was looking straight in my direction as he gripped his steering wheel with both hands. He was about twenty feet from my window.

Then, complete silence.

I was amazed that I was not knocked off my feet, moved from where I was standing after jumping back, or hit by any flying debris. It was absolutely miraculous. I was spared.

About two seconds after all this, I remembered Josh was on the phone. He had listened to the entire thing. When I asked him later if I had said anything before the crash, he told me that he heard me say (not yell!), "Oh my gosh." I don't remember saying that, but I must have, as I saw the car coming at me. I put the phone back to my ear and said, "Josh, a car just came through the wall of my office. Call your mother and tell her to call 911." Then I hung up.

I remember quickly looking down at my feet, which were buried in rubble. And then I realized how fortunate I was. I gratefully muttered, "Thank you for sparing my life." I immediately heard the yells of numerous witnesses who had seen what happened and were running to the hole in my office wall. I heard one man yelling to the driver, "Are you all right? Are you all right?" I stretched my neck to look out the hole and was surprised to see that the man yelling to the driver was one of my neighbors, who had been in his car at the time of the accident and had narrowly missed being hit. I saw him and said, "Oh, hey Ron," while waving at him. His eyes got as big as pancakes and he said, "OH MY GOSH, WALT! WERE YOU IN THERE? ARE YOU OK? I CAN'T BELIEVE YOU'RE OK!"

Concerned that there might be flammable fluids leaking from the car, I kept telling the driver—who was in a state of dumbfounded shock and surrounded by air bags—"You have to get out of the car. You have to get out of the car." I turned around and opened the other office window and took out the screen. I still don't know how the driver got out of his car, but he followed me out the window.

> **Five minutes after climbing out the window, my knees started shaking, and I got tears in my eyes as my wife and kids showed up and I saw the looks on their faces.**

It took about five minutes for me to really realize what had happened. To my surprise I had remained calm, even-keeled, eyes open, had never screamed, never yelled—perhaps because it all happened so fast. Then, five minutes after climbing out the window, my knees started shaking, and I got tears in my eyes as my wife and kids showed up and I saw the looks on their faces.

At this point, we still don't know what happened. The driver may have fallen asleep at the wheel. The noises I had heard just before the crash were from his car fishtailing at a high speed and knocking down signs as he careened down the road.

> I actually came into the office alone last night
> and stood outside my door looking in,
> thanking God for sparing me from death and injury.

The miracle of it all for me is that the only thing I found on my body were abrasions around both knees, probably from flying debris. In addition, large pieces of splintered furniture that had been on my right-hand side when I stood up were all directly on my left-hand side after it was over. They either passed through me or took a "magic bullet" turn around me before landing.

Could it have been God's hand in all this? Absolutely!

For insurance purposes I was instructed to go to the doctor. He cleaned out the abrasions and gave me a tetanus shot. That's it.

Why are we sharing all this? We want to thank you for your prayers for CPYU. God's hand was on me in a big way yesterday. I actually came into the office alone last night and stood outside my door looking in, thanking God for sparing me from death and injury.

Continue to keep us in your prayers. We're a bit out of sorts here with lots of cleanup and insurance work to tend to, as you can imagine. All this comes at a time when our speaking schedule is kicking off, and I'm working to complete some writing.

Thanks again for your continued prayers. And thanks be to God for his hand in our lives.

Opie Doesn't Live Here Anymore

MOURNING TO DANCING

Blog; November 24, 2003

Last night I stood in the wide hallway of the St. Louis Convention Center with my wife, Lisa, Marv Penner and his wife, Lois, and Youth Specialties' Tic Long. Just on the other side of the wall, five thousand convention attendees were immersed in the Passion Worship Experience. The four of us surrounded Tic and stared into his tired eyes as he walked us through the whirlwind that's been his life since we saw him last month in Charlotte.

> **Tic couldn't stop talking about God's fingerprint on it all. He had seen God work in the midst of all the craziness.**

Tic described how his house in the California hills had been miraculously spared from fiery destruction three times. Just when he was catching his breath, he learned of the death of his good friend, Mike Yaconelli. That was the start of two weeks of grief, joy, memorials, questioning, crying, and trying to sort it all out. Then, Tic and his YS crew converged on St. Louis to pull off the last of the three 2003 conventions. It was his fiftieth YS conference—he had done the first forty-nine with Mike— and there he stood, on the convention's last night . . . looking drained.

Still, Tic couldn't stop talking about God's fingerprint on it all. He excitedly jumped from this to that, to this to that—all the while describing how he had seen God work in the midst of all the craziness. When our time with Tic was up, I couldn't help thinking about the greatness of

God—how in his grace he turns our sorrow into joy and our mourning into gladness (Jeremiah 31:13).

Somehow that truth will be realized by the youth-worker couple who—just minutes before we started chatting with Tic—were kneeling in grief on the hallway floor. The joy of being at the convention was interrupted by a phone call telling them that two of their students had just been killed in a car accident. Just a few days before, another of their students had died suddenly from heart failure.

> **Even while I've been scribbling this, Josh called to tell me "Dad, I'm on my way home" from the funeral of a friend.**

Somehow, I trust that truth also will be realized by my seventeen-year-old son, Josh. Even while I've been scribbling this, Josh called to tell me "Dad, I'm on my way home" from the funeral of a friend. Two of his friends lost their lives in a nasty accident last Thursday night. Sorrow into joy, and mourning into gladness . . .

Thanks, Tic, for leading me, Lisa, Marv, and Lois in our own little worship service right there under the bright lights of that sterile convention center. Josh will be walking through the door in a few minutes, and I'll go downstairs to chat with him about the funeral. I trust that somehow, some way, our little late-night chat will lead him to gain a deeper glimpse of his creator.

Opie Doesn't Live Here Anymore

SEASONED VET

Blog; March 22, 2004

I was reminded this weekend of the fact that I'm dying—and you are too.

The reality that death is a fact of life hit me again as I watched the place where I had made so many memories crumble into dust over a span of sixty-two seconds. I spent many afternoons and nights in Philadelphia's Veterans Stadium over the course of my teenage and young adult years. That's where I watched the Phillies, the Eagles, and even a couple of professional soccer games. While watching the live TV coverage of the stadium's implosion, I got to thinking about the fact that either I was fooling myself that the stadium wasn't that old, or I was fooling myself that I'm not that old. But then reality hit.

I was fourteen when the stadium first opened. I had already spent many years watching the Phils play at old Connie Mack Stadium. I was sad when they ripped that place down. It felt like some of my childhood was gone. Now I'm old enough to have seen my team wear out two stadiums and move on to a third!

> I got to thinking about the fact that either I was fooling myself that the stadium wasn't that old, or I was fooling myself that I'm not that old. But then reality hit.

I tried to console myself with the fact that we live in an era of rapid change. That's true—so we shouldn't be surprised that the Vet only lasted about thirty-four years. But the fact also is that I am getting older. And just like the pile of dust and rubble sitting in South Philly that once was the Vet, my body is experiencing the decay that's come into the world as a result of my sin. Of course, I do try to take care of myself by exercising several days a week. But I'm only fooling myself if I believe that I can stop the aging process and prevent my death—it's a losing battle.

Many in our society think otherwise. I overhead a conversation at the gym just two days ago that was pretty sad. A young man mentioned that he was working out so he doesn't ever realize his fear that his wife will stop finding him attractive. Hmmmm. I'm wondering why she married him.

> **This message doesn't just serve to give me hope, it serves to keep me pushing on in my efforts to see the kids we know and love clothed with the imperishable.**

My thoughts on watching the Vet crumble also got me thinking about our upcoming Easter celebration. Yes, some day the blood will stop flowing through my body, my heart will stop beating, and this thing I look at in the mirror every morning will be reduced to dust. But thanks be to God for the hope of the resurrection! The apostle Paul wrote some amazingly encouraging truths to the Corinthians: "When the perishable has been clothed with the imperishable, and the mortal with immortality, then the saying that is written will come true: 'Death has been swallowed up in victory.' 'Where, O death, is your victory? Where, O death, is your sting?'" (1 Corinthians 15:54, 55).

Opie Doesn't Live Here Anymore

This message doesn't just serve to give me hope, it serves to keep me pushing on in my efforts to see the kids we know and love clothed with the imperishable.

EMBRACING THE COLLISION

Though he slay me, yet will I hope in him. (Job 13:15)

Let him who walks in the dark, who has no light, trust in the name of the Lord and rely on his God. (Isaiah 50:10)

I will never leave you nor forsake you. (Joshua 1:5)

And surely I am with you always, to the very end of the age. (Matthew 28:20)

The heavens declare the glory of God; the skies proclaim the works of his hands. (Psalm 19:1)

1. "GOD, WHERE ARE YOU?" Have you ever cried out to God with those words? Why is this an important prayer for us to pray?

2. HAVE YOU EVER LET life's normal circumstances keep you from seeing evidence of the greatness of God and his world in the little things? What steps can you take to see more of God in the smaller details of life?

3. WHY IS THE REALITY that death is a fact of life difficult for us to deal with? What are some ways we try to avoid the truth of that fact?

4. HOW DOES 1 CORINTHIANS 15:54, 55 provide comfort in the face of that reality?

Is God Near?

ABOUT WALT MUELLER

 **WALT MUELLER IS THE FOUNDER AND PRESIDENT** of the Center for Parent/Youth Understanding (www.cpyu.org), based in Elizabethtown, Pennsylvania—a nearly two-decade-old, nonprofit ministry organization serving churches, schools, and community organizations across the U.S., Canada, and worldwide. CPYU's goal is to communicate the gospel cross-culturally by helping those who know and love children, teens, and college-age students to understand today's rapidly changing youth culture.

Walt has been working with young people and families for more than thirty years, including serving in youth ministry with the Coalition for Christian Outreach and as a youth pastor in churches in Johnstown, Pennsylvania, and in Philadelphia.

Through CPYU, he has become an internationally recognized speaker and author on contemporary youth culture. He's provided commentary for numerous international media outlets, including CNN, Fox News, and the BBC, and can be heard on more than 800 radio stations across the United States and Canada on CPYU's daily radio spot, *Youth Culture Today.*

He has written extensively on youth culture and family issues and is the author of several books, including *Youth Culture 101* (Zondervan, 2007); *I Want to Talk with My Teen About Movies, Music & More* (Standard Publishing,

2006); *Engaging the Soul of Youth Culture: Bridging Teen Worldviews and Christian Truth* (InterVarsity Press, 2006); and the critically acclaimed Gold Medallion Award winner, *Understanding Today's Youth Culture* (Tyndale House, 1994). He's also a regular contributor to numerous journals and magazines, including *YouthWorker Journal* and *Living with Teenagers*.

A graduate of Geneva College (BA) and Gordon-Conwell Theological Seminary (MDiv), Walt completed his doctorate at Gordon-Conwell in "Ministry to Postmodern Generations."

Walt and his wife, Lisa, live in Elizabethtown and have four children.

Opie Doesn't Live Here Anymore

NOTES

INTRODUCTION

1. John Piper, *A Godward Life: Savoring the Supremacy of God in All of Life* (Sisters, Ore.: Multnomah, 1997), 85.

LOOKING FOR BUS #119—ON YOUTH CULTURE AND MORALS

1. Mary Pipher, *Reviving Ophelia: Saving the Selves of Adolescent Girls* (New York: Ballentine Books, 1994), 184.

2. Joan Jacobs Brumberg, *The Body Project: An Intimate History of American Girls* (New York: Vintage, 1998), xx, xxi.

3. Sara Shandler, *Ophelia Speaks: Adolescent Girls Write About Their Search for Self* (New York: Harper Perennial, 1999), 5.

4. Jean Kilbourne, *Deadly Persuasion: Why Women and Girls Must Fight the Addictive Power of Advertising* (New York: The Free Press, 1999), 134.

5. Sheila Rayman, "Girls Precocious but Unprepared," *USA Today*, September 13, 2000, 8D.

6. Kendall Payne, "Supermodels," from *Jordan's Sister*, Capitol Records, 1999.

7. I would add to Stott's comment, "And in the lives of the children, teens, and young adults of today!"

8. John R.W. Stott, *Between Two Worlds: The Art of Preaching in the Twentieth Century* (Grand Rapids, Mich.: Eerdmans, 1982), 137, 138.

9. John R.W. Stott, *The Contemporary Christian: Applying God's Word to Today's World* (Downers Grove, Ill.: InterVarsity Press, 1992), 110, 111.

10. Neale Donald Walsch, *Conversations with God for Teens* (Charlottesville, Va.: Hampton Roads Publishing Co., 2001), 13.

11. Ibid., 91.

12. John White, *The Fight: A Practical Handbook to Christian Living* (Downers Grove, Ill.: InterVarsity Press, 1976), 61.

On Love and Life

1. Anne Lamott, *Traveling Mercies: Some Thoughts on Faith* (New York: Random House, 1999), 100.

Desperate Times, Divine Measures

1. Marvin Gaye, "What's Going On," from *What's Going On*, Motown Records, 1971.

2. George Barna, *Generation Next: What You Need to Know About Today's Youth* (Ventura, Calif.: Regal Books, 1996), 31ff.

3. Creed, "In America," from *My Own Prison*, Wind-up Records, 1997.

Opie Doesn't Live Here Anymore

4. Sheryl Crow, "Everyday is a Winding Road," from *Sheryl Crow*, A&M Records, 1996.

THE WORLD PULLED OVER OUR EYES

1. "Morpheus' Proposal," *The Matrix*, DVD, directed by Andy Wachowski and Larry Wachowski (1999, Warner Home Video).

2. Grant Wahl, *Sports Illustrated*, 1999, http://sportsillustrated.cnn.com/features/1999/sportsman/archive/wahl/

3. Bill Dwyre, "Crossing the Line," *Los Angeles Times*, July 15, 1999, D1.

4. Jonathan Margolis, "Tangled Webs for Sale," *Time Magazine Europe*, Vol. 155, No. 23, June 12, 2000, http://www.time.com/time/europe/magazine/2000/0612/lies.html

5. Michael Moore, *Cheating 101: The Benefits and Fundamentals of Earning the Easy A* (Hopewell, N.J.: Moore Publishing, 1991).

6. The Center for Academic Integrity, "The Fundamental Values of Academic Integrity," October 1999, 1.

7. Betty Ann Bowser, "Cheating Teachers," *Online Newshour*, April 26, 2000, http://www.pbs.org/newshour/bb/education/jan-june2000/teachers_4-26.html

8. George Barna, *Generation Next: What You Need to Know About Today's Youth* (Ventura, Calif.: Regal Books, 1996), 47.

9. Thomas Lickona, *Educating for Character: How Our Schools Can Teach Respect and Responsibility* (New York: Bantam Books, 1991), 57.

10. "High-Tech Cheating in Schools," MSNBC interview published on ZDNet.com, February 18, 1999, http://news.zdnet.com/2100-9595_22-513776.html

11. Erik Hedegaard, "There's Something About Virgins," *Rolling Stone*, August 19, 1999, http://www.rollingstone.com/news/story/5931700

12. Tom Beaudoin, *Virtual Faith: The Irreverent Spiritual Quest of Generation X* (San Francisco: Jossey-Bass, 1998), 25.

13. Tom Conroy and Rob Sheffield, "Hot Image Makeover," *Rolling Stone*, August 19, 1999, 3C.

14. Barna, *Generation Next: What You Need to Know About Today's Youth*, 76.

15. Steven Daley, "Inside the Bedroom of America's New Teen Queen," *Rolling Stone*, April 15, 1999, http://www.rollingstone.com/news/story/5939508

Rethinking: How We Do Christianity

1. Christian Smith with Melinda Lundquist Denton, *Soul Searching: The Religious and Spiritual Lives of American Teenagers* (New York, NY: Oxford University Press, 2005), 162, 163.

Opie Doesn't Live Here Anymore

2. Os Guinness, *Unspeakable: Facing Up to Evil in an Age of Genocide and Terror* (New York: HarperSanFrancisco, 2005), 91.

3. Marva Dawn, *Reaching Out Without Dumbing Down: A Theology of Worship for the Turn-of-the-Century Culture* (Grand Rapids, Mich.: Wm. B. Eerdmans, 1995), 280.

4. Ibid., 282.

5. Lyrics are from the hymn "Holy, Holy, Holy! Lord God Almighty," by Reginald Heber.

6. Dean Borgman, *When Kumbaya Is Not Enough: A Practical Theology for Youth Ministry* (Peabody, Mass.: Hendrickson Publishers, 1997), 16.

7. Charles Colson, *Loving God* (Grand Rapids, Mich.: Zondervan, 1983), 127.

8. John R. W. Stott, *Christ the Controversialist* (Downers Grove, Ill.: InterVarsity Press, 1970), 191.

9. Kenneth Kantzer, "Ron Sider Is Mostly Right," *Christianity Today*, October 8, 1990, 21.

10. Tom Sine, "Will the Real Cultural Christian Please Stand Up," *World Vision Magazine*, October/November 1989, 21.

11. Gary Gilley, *I Just Wanted More Land—Jabez: A Careful Analysis of Bruce Wilkinson's Best-Selling Book, 'The Prayer of Jabez'* (Longwood, Fla.: Xulon Press, 2002).

12. Ronald J. Sider, *The Scandal of the Evangelical Conscience: Why Are Christians Living Just Like the Rest of the World?* (Grand Rapids, Mich.: Baker Books, 2005), 85; 12, 13.

13. C.S. Lewis, *The Screwtape Letters*, copyright © C.S. Lewis Pte. Ltd. 1942. Extract reprinted by permission.

14. Gordon T. Smith, *Beginning Well: Christian Conversion & Authentic Transformation* (Downers Grove, Ill.: InterVarsity Press, 2001), 135.

15. Dallas Willard, *The Divine Conspiracy: Rediscovering Our Hidden Life in God* (New York: InterVarsity Press, 1998), 35ff.

16. David Wells, "The Bleeding of the Evangelical Church," *Banner of Truth Magazine*, 1996, http://www.founders.org/FJ63/article3.html

Is God Near?

1. Timothy White, "Johnny Carson: The Rolling Stone Interview," *Rolling Stone*, originally published March 22, 1979, www.rollingstone.com/news/story/6862856

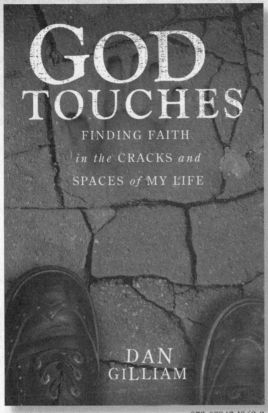

Do You Feel Like A Visitor In Your Own Skin?

Maybe you have spiritual amnesia. You've forgotten your spiritual identity. Perhaps you've bought into the myth that you exist only to eat, sleep, work, pay your bills, and be a good citizen. But to know why you're here, you have to know who you are. Understanding your identity is crucial to fulfilling your destiny.

ARRON CHAMBERS
REMEMBER WHO YOU ARE

releasing the power of an identity-driven life

Inside *Remember Who You Are* you'll discover:
You Are Not Ordinary • You Were Created On Purpose
You Are Free • You Are Loved • You Are An Overcomer
. . . And A Whole Lot More!

24324 • 9780784720055

Maybe it's time to forget who you've become and remember who you are!

To purchase visit your local Christian bookstore or find it online at www.standardpub.com.